HOMOSEXUALITY

Opposing Viewpoints®

OTHER BOOKS OF RELATED INTEREST

HOMOSEXUALITY

Opposing Viewpoints®

Mary E. Williams, Book Editor

18042

David L. Bender, *Publisher*
Bruno Leone, *Executive Editor*
Bonnie Szumski, *Editorial Director*
David M. Haugen, *Managing Editor*

OPPOSING
VIEWPOINTS®
SERIES

Greenhaven Press, Inc., San Diego, California

Library of Congress Cataloging-in-Publication Data

Homosexuality : opposing viewpoints / Mary E. Williams, book editor.
    p.   cm. — (Opposing viewpoints series)
    Includes bibliographical references and index.
    ISBN 0-7377-0053-X (lib. : alk. paper). —
  ISBN 0-7377-0052-1 (pbk. : alk. paper)
    1. Homosexuality—United States. 2. Gays—United States.
  I. Williams, Mary E., 1960–   . II. Series: Opposing viewpoints series
  (Unnumbered)
  HQ76.3.U5H675 1999
  305.9'0664—dc21   98-32020
                                                           CIP

Greenhaven Press, Inc., P.O. Box 289009
San Diego, CA 92198-9009

"CONGRESS SHALL MAKE NO LAW...ABRIDGING THE FREEDOM OF SPEECH, OR OF THE PRESS."

First Amendment to the U.S. Constitution

The basic foundation of our democracy is the First Amendment guarantee of freedom of expression. The Opposing Viewpoints Series is dedicated to the concept of this basic freedom and the idea that it is more important to practice it than to enshrine it.

CONTENTS

Chapter 4: Should Society Sanction Gay and Lesbian Families?

WHY CONSIDER
OPPOSING VIEWPOINTS?

"The only way in which a human being can make some approach to knowing the whole of a subject is by hearing what can be said about it by persons of every variety of opinion and studying all modes in which it can be looked at by every character of mind. No wise man ever acquired his wisdom in any mode but this."

John Stuart Mill

In our media-intensive culture it is not difficult to find differing opinions. Thousands of newspapers and magazines and dozens of radio and television talk shows resound with differing points of view. The difficulty lies in deciding which opinion to agree with and which "experts" seem the most credible. The more inundated we become with differing opinions and claims, the more essential it is to hone critical reading and thinking skills to evaluate these ideas. Opposing Viewpoints books address this problem directly by presenting stimulating debates that can be used to enhance and teach these skills. The varied opinions contained in each book examine many different aspects of a single issue. While examining these conveniently edited opposing views, readers can develop critical thinking skills such as the ability to compare and contrast authors' credibility, facts, argumentation styles, use of persuasive techniques, and other stylistic tools. In short, the Opposing Viewpoints Series is an ideal way to attain the higher-level thinking and reading skills so essential in a culture of diverse and contradictory opinions.

In addition to providing a tool for critical thinking, Opposing Viewpoints books challenge readers to question their own strongly held opinions and assumptions. Most people form their opinions on the basis of upbringing, peer pressure, and personal, cultural, or professional bias. By reading carefully balanced opposing views, readers must directly confront new ideas as well as the opinions of those with whom they disagree. This is not to simplistically argue that everyone who reads opposing views will—or should—change his or her opinion. Instead, the series enhances readers' understanding of their own views by encouraging confrontation with opposing ideas. Careful examination of others' views can lead to the readers' understanding of the logical inconsistencies in their own opinions, perspective on why they hold an opinion, and the consideration of the possibility that their opinion requires further evaluation.

EVALUATING OTHER OPINIONS

To ensure that this type of examination occurs, Opposing Viewpoints books present all types of opinions. Prominent spokespeople on different sides of each issue as well as well-known professionals from many disciplines challenge the reader. An additional goal of the series is to provide a forum for other, less known, or even unpopular viewpoints. The opinion of an ordinary person who has had to make the decision to cut off life support from a terminally ill relative, for example, may be just as valuable and provide just as much insight as a medical ethicist's professional opinion. The editors have two additional purposes in including these less known views. One, the editors encourage readers to respect others' opinions—even when not enhanced by professional credibility. It is only by reading or listening to and objectively evaluating others' ideas that one can determine whether they are worthy of consideration. Two, the inclusion of such viewpoints encourages the important critical thinking skill of objectively evaluating an author's credentials and bias. This evaluation will illuminate an author's reasons for taking a particular stance on an issue and will aid in readers' evaluation of the author's ideas.

As series editors of the Opposing Viewpoints Series, it is our hope that these books will give readers a deeper understanding of the issues debated and an appreciation of the complexity of even seemingly simple issues when good and honest people disagree. This awareness is particularly important in a democratic society such as ours in which people enter into public debate to determine the common good. Those with whom one disagrees should not be regarded as enemies but rather as people whose views deserve careful examination and may shed light on one's own.

Thomas Jefferson once said that "difference of opinion leads to inquiry, and inquiry to truth." Jefferson, a broadly educated man, argued that "if a nation expects to be ignorant and free . . . it expects what never was and never will be." As individuals and as a nation, it is imperative that we consider the opinions of others and examine them with skill and discernment. The Opposing Viewpoints Series is intended to help readers achieve this goal.

David L. Bender & Bruno Leone,
Series Editors

Greenhaven Press anthologies primarily consist of previously published material taken from a variety of sources, including periodicals, books, scholarly journals, newspapers, government documents, and position papers from private and public organizations. These original sources are often edited for length and to ensure their accessibility for a young adult audience. The anthology editors also change the original titles of these works in order to clearly present the main thesis of each viewpoint and to explicitly indicate the opinion presented in the viewpoint. These alterations are made in consideration of both the reading and comprehension levels of a young adult audience. Every effort is made to ensure that Greenhaven Press accurately reflects the original intent of the authors included in this anthology.

INTRODUCTION

"More than 100 Christian ministries to homosexuals help those who are seeking a way out of homosexuality."
—Alan P. Medinger

"There is no evidence that any treatment can change a homosexual person's deep seated sexual feelings for others of the same sex."
—American Psychiatric Association

On June 15, 1998, Republican senator Trent Lott stirred controversy when he discussed his opinions on homosexuality in a taped interview conducted by Armstrong Williams for America's Voice, a cable television network. Lott declared that homosexuality is "a sin" and a pathology comparable to alcoholism, sex addiction, and kleptomania. Homosexuals should not be mistreated or rejected, Lott insisted; instead, they should be shown "a way to deal with" homosexuality.

Then on July 13, 1998, Exodus International—a religious outreach organization that agrees with Lott's views on homosexuality—launched a major advertising campaign. With financial support from several conservative groups, Exodus International took out full-page ads in major newspapers to proclaim that homosexuals could become heterosexual through ministry and therapy. Many of the ads feature Anne Paulk, a self-described "wife, mother, and former lesbian" who contends that her previous life as a homosexual was the result of childhood sexual abuse. After renewing her relationship with God and undergoing counseling with Exodus International, Paulk maintains, she walked away from her homosexual identity. Paulk encourages other gay people to "begin the real road to healing" by contacting one of the various "ex-gay" ministries.

Lott's comments and Exodus International's ads provoked outrage from many gays and lesbians and their supporters. In doing so, they reignited the debate over the causes of homosexuality and over how homosexuals should be viewed and treated by society. For much of American history, homosexuality has been condemned as a form of immoral behavior or as a mental disorder. In 1973, however, the American Psychiatric Association removed homosexuality from its list of mental illnesses and advocated the elimination of discrimination against gays and lesbians.

By the early 1990s, several scientists claimed to have discovered some evidence of a biological basis for homosexuality: In 1991, neurobiologist Simon LeVay published results from a study revealing a connection between brain structure and homosexuality; during that same year, psychologists Michael Bailey and Richard Pillard presented surveys of families suggesting that homosexuality was an inherited trait. In 1993, researcher Dean Hamer announced that he had discovered a genetic factor linked to male homosexuality. These findings reinforce the belief among many advocates for gays and lesbians that homosexuality is innate and, therefore, a psychologically normal variation of human behavior.

Critics of the recent scientific findings, however, point out that follow-up studies have not confirmed the theory that homosexuality is biologically determined. Many of these critics argue that environmental factors such as childhood sexual abuse or dysfunctional parent-child relationships can result in a homosexual orientation. The ex-gay outreach ministries, as well as secular organizations such as the National Association for Research and Therapy of Homosexuality (NARTH), are among those who maintain that homosexuality is an environmentally determined—and treatable—pathology.

Founded in 1976, Exodus International is one of the most well known ex-gay ministries, with eighty-three chapters in thirty-five states. Its national board chairman, John Paulk, is an ex-gay and former drag queen who is now married to Anne Paulk, the ex-lesbian featured in the ministry's first full-page newspaper ads. John Paulk contends that his homosexuality stemmed from "a continuous insecurity" he experienced while growing up without a father. As he developed, he argues, his unfulfilled need for masculine influence evolved into a sexual attraction to other males. Only after a discussion with a college pastor did Paulk come to the conclusion that he had not been born gay. Then, with the help of Exodus International, Paulk was able to abandon his homosexual lifestyle by making a daily commitment to serve Jesus Christ: "In the past, I could never say, 'I'm a man.' But now I'm a different person, 'a new creature in Christ.' I can be loved just because I'm his."

While Exodus International emphasizes Christ-centered ministry and counseling, NARTH offers a referral service of licensed therapists who provide "reparative therapy"—psychological treatment for homosexuals who wish to change their sexual orientation. These psychologists use group therapy, one-on-one counseling, and behavior modification techniques to help homosexuals change, maintains NARTH executive director Joseph

Nicolosi. According to a 1997 survey of 860 individuals undergoing reparative therapy, "only 13 percent perceived themselves as . . . homosexual" after treatment, NARTH contends.

Critics of ex-gay counseling and reparative therapy, however, dispute claims that gays can "convert" to heterosexuality. For one thing, research psychologist Gregory M. Herek points out, a significant problem in "many published reports of 'successful' conversion therapies is that the participants' initial sexual orientation was never adequately assessed. Many bisexuals have been mislabeled as homosexuals with the consequence that the 'successes' reported . . . actually have occurred among bisexuals who were motivated to adopt a heterosexual behavior pattern." Furthermore, Herek and others argue, attempts to change a gay person's sexual orientation are harmful and unethical. According to psychologists Ariel Shidlo and Michael Schroeder, who conducted interviews with gay people who unsuccessfully tried to change their sexual orientation, "a significant proportion of reparative therapy patients sustain serious, lasting injuries." Some therapies, they maintain, use electric shocks or nausea-producing drugs to quell same-sex attraction and end up reducing patients' capacity for sexual feelings and intimacy. Many patients become depressed when a "cure" eludes them, putting them at higher risk for such self-destructive behaviors as drug abuse and suicide attempts, Shidlo asserts. Moreover, he reports, family relationships are often damaged by counselors who insist that homosexuality results from poor parenting. In response to ethical concerns about so-called conversion therapies, the American Psychological Association (APA) passed a 1997 resolution opposing "all portrayals of lesbian, gay, and bisexual people as mentally ill and in need of treatment due to their sexual orientation." The APA maintains that gay people who wish to become straight are suffering from self-hatred brought on by society's aversion to homosexuality. Those in agreement with the APA contend that the healthiest counseling for troubled gays and lesbians is therapy that emphasizes self-acceptance, not conversion.

Clearly, the subject of homosexuality continues to generate heartfelt differences of opinion. *Homosexuality: Opposing Viewpoints* examines several deeply contentious topics in the following chapters: What Causes Homosexuality? Do Homosexuals Face Serious Discrimination? Should Society Encourage Increased Acceptance of Homosexuality? Should Society Sanction Gay and Lesbian Families? The viewpoints presented here demonstrate that homosexuality will remain a prominent and controversial issue in the American social and political arena.

CHAPTER 1

WHAT CAUSES HOMOSEXUALITY?

CHAPTER PREFACE

The question of what causes some people to be sexually attracted to members of their own gender has generated several theories. These theories tend to reflect the classic debate on whether a person's makeup is the product of biology or environment. Some researchers contend that homosexuality is the result of environmental factors such as a child's relationship to his or her parents or experiences of childhood sexual abuse. Others argue that homosexuality is genetically or biologically determined—a consequence of genes, prenatal hormonal influences, or variations in brain structure. Still others maintain that same-sex attraction stems from an unpredictable combination of biological and environmental factors.

These debates about causation have important political implications for gays and lesbians. Some believe that if homosexuality is proven to be the result of genetics or biology, society will come to accept same-sex attraction as natural, and antigay sentiment and discrimination will decrease. Simon LeVay, the neurobiologist who claimed in 1991 to have discovered a link between brain structure and homosexuality, contends that "the biological findings reinforce what most gays and lesbians feel about themselves—that their sexual orientation is something given, an attribute that helps define their core identity, not a mere set of behaviours that a person chooses to engage in or not as whim or morality may dictate."

Others are not so sure whether evidence demonstrating physical causes of homosexuality would have such a favorable impact on society's attitudes toward homosexuals. Lesbian journalist Erin Blades argues that "confirmation of a genetic cause for homosexuality won't change people's attitudes toward gay people. . . . What makes us think that given how cruel and punitive so many have been toward us that [a] gay gene won't be seen as pathological?" Those who agree with Blades fear that the discovery of biological causes could even lead to efforts to "cure" homosexuality through brain-cell transplants, corrective hormonal injections, or genetic engineering.

Clearly, the source of same-sex attraction is of more than scientific interest—it is an issue that may have social repercussions as well. The viewpoints in the following chapter examine several theories on the causes of homosexuality.

1

"Homosexuality is not a personal choice, a mental disorder or a learned perversion . . . it is a natural genetic condition."

HOMOSEXUALITY IS BIOLOGICALLY DETERMINED

Steve Kangas

In the following viewpoint, Steve Kangas argues that homosexuality is a biologically inherited condition. Scientific research of homosexual brothers has identified several genetic markers in a region of the X chromosome that may comprise all or part of a gay gene, the author points out. Other surveys have revealed that there is a higher than average occurrence of homosexual orientation among siblings and twins of homosexuals, suggesting that homosexuality runs in families, Kangas contends. These scientific findings prove that homosexuality is a naturally occurring state of being; gay people therefore deserve societal acceptance and respect, Kangas concludes. Kangas is a former editor for *Suite 101.com*, an on-line journal and informational guide to the World Wide Web.

As you read, consider the following questions:

1. According to Kangas, what evidence suggests that homosexuality is not the result of parental conditioning?
2. What is genetic "penetrance," according to Kangas?
3. In the author's opinion, what facts prove that the National Association for Research and Therapy of Homosexuality (NARTH) is a disreputable organization?

Reprinted from Steve Kangas, "Gay Politics, Gay Science," web article dated November 7, 1997, at www.suite101.com/articles/article.cfm/4085.

W ith gay rights back in the news, this is a good time to review the state of gay politics and gay science.

In November 1997, President Bill Clinton will attend a gay
rights fund-raising dinner, where lesbian actress Ellen De-
Generes (of the TV sitcom *Ellen*) will receive a civil rights award.
That the president would feel no political risk for attending such
an event is in remarkable contrast to the controversy that ex-
ploded in 1993 when he attempted to legalize gays in the military. That move, although morally correct, was a political blun-
der of the first order, giving conservatives an early stick to beat
him with, and cutting short his proverbial honeymoon with the
nation.

A SHIFT IN PUBLIC ATTITUDES

But the president's attendance at a major gay-rights dinner is
symbolic of a larger trend. By nearly all indicators, gay political
life is improving. In the last few years, public attitudes against
gays have become more accepting and open-minded. According
to the ongoing General Social Survey, between 1973 and 1993
the number of Americans who considered homosexuality to be
"always wrong" always exceeded 66 percent. But since 1993
this number has been falling, to 56.5 percent by 1996. Gallup
polls reflect the same trend. In 1982, 51 percent of all Americans believed that homosexuality is not an acceptable lifestyle,
compared to 34 percent who thought it is. By 1996, however,
those opposed fell to 50 percent, while those accepting rose to
44 percent. According to demographic analysis, those who are
more accepting of gays tend to be young, educated, liberal, secular, female and/or personally acquainted with a gay person.

What is responsible for this growing shift in public opinions?
Certainly President Clinton deserves some credit for bringing
gay issues to the national debate, as well as hiring prominent gay
federal officials like Roberta Achtenberg and Virginia Apuzzo. But
an even more important reason is that science is finally laying to
rest old superstitions, beliefs and stereotypes about homosexuality. In the growing mountain of scientific evidence, undoubtedly
the most important is the confirmation that homosexuality is
not a personal choice, a mental disorder or a learned perversion
. . . it is a natural genetic condition.

HOMOSEXUALITY IS GENETIC

Science is only confirming what many observers have long de-
duced. The vast majority of gays has long reported that they
knew their orientation from the onset of adolescence or even

earlier, just like heterosexuals. Given the clear genetic basis of hormones and sexual attraction, this suggests that homosexuality is genetic too.

Furthermore, homosexuality runs in the family. Critics argue this is because parents condition their children to become gay, but the facts do not bear out this claim. If the "conditioning" thesis is correct, we would expect homosexuality to occur in these families randomly. But in fact it occurs far more frequently on the mother's side of the extended family than the father's. Today we know why: the gay gene occurs on the mother's X chromosome, on a segment where it is impervious to natural selection. (This is why homosexuality is not bred out of the gene pool, as you might expect.)

Also striking is the fact that the rate of homosexuality appears to be constant all over the globe, regardless of how tolerant or intolerant any particular society is. Homosexuality is also seen everywhere in countless animal species—how "culture" could produce such behavior is a good question. Archbishop Benjamin Tutu of South Africa probably makes the most cogent argument here:

> Someone has said that if this sexual orientation were indeed a matter of personal choice, then homosexual persons must be the craziest coots around to choose a way of life that exposes them to so much hostility, discrimination, loss and suffering.

SCIENTIFIC RESEARCH

Lately, science has corroborated the idea that homosexuality is genetic. Researcher Dean Hamer compared the DNA of 40 pairs of homosexual brothers and found that 33 shared genetic markers in the Xq28 region of their X chromosome. This may be either all or part of a "gay gene." (Often so-called "single" traits are determined at several different points on the DNA strand.)

Psychologists Michael Bailey and Richard Pillard have studied identical twins raised together. They found that when one twin is gay, there is a 52 percent chance the other will be too. (The actual rate is probably higher, due to the stigma of admitting to be gay, even to a researcher.) For fraternal twins, the chance is only 22 percent, and for non-twin or adopted siblings, only 10 percent.

Critics of these tests argue that if homosexuality is half genetic, then it must be half environmental as well, and this proves that social factors and personal choice must be involved in becoming gay. But this is a serious misunderstanding of how genes work. Genes have a trait called "penetrance," which is the chance that a gene will become activated. The gene for Huntington's Disease comes in two varieties, or alleles. One allele suppresses the disease, the other activates it. The latter is 100 percent penetrant, meaning that if you have this allele, you are 100 percent certain to come down with the disease. By contrast, the allele activating the gene for Type 1 diabetes is only 30 percent penetrant. In other words, there is only a 30 percent chance this gene will become activated. (But if activated, diabetes is certain.) Therefore, two identical twins could share the same gene for diabetes, but only one might develop it. The penetrance of the gay gene appears to be 50 percent, which is why some twins do not share the same sexual orientation. Incidentally, no one knows what triggers this allele, but all evidence indicates that it is triggered in the womb or early childhood—too early for the person to make a "choice."

THE SECRETS OF HOMOPHOBIA

Science is not only uncovering the secrets of homosexuality, but homophobia as well. In 1996, a team of researchers led by Dr. Henry Adams conducted an experiment on 64 white men, all of whom were straight in both their sexual and fantasy life. The researchers rated 35 as homophobic and 29 as non-homophobic. Using a device called a *plethysmograph*, the researchers measured their sexual arousal while viewing pornographic films. During films that showed sex between men and women, all the subjects showed the same rates of arousal. However, during films that showed sex between men only, 54 percent of the homophobic men showed definite signs of arousal, compared to only 24 percent of the non-homophobic men. The researchers concluded that homophobia probably represents repressed homosexuality in these men.

Recently, groups like the National Association for Research and Therapy of Homosexuality (NARTH) have been promoting "reparation" therapy, wherein gay people undergo counseling and therapy "to become heterosexual again." These groups are usually Christian conservative organizations practicing crank science. They do not participate in academic conferences, publish in peer-reviewed journals, or otherwise take part in the academic mainstream. Instead, they publish their dubious studies on the Internet and "debate" via press releases. NARTH itself is a tiny organization with only six officers, which appears to be the limit of its doctoral membership.

The American Psychological Association (APA), by contrast, has 151,000 professional members and is the world's largest and most prestigious organization representing psychologists. Among its many duties is assembling panels of the world's best psychologists to review matters of controversy and to critique and assess all research relating to such issues. Recently, the APA overwhelmingly passed a resolution condemning reparative therapy. It strongly opposed classifying gay people as mentally ill or suffering from psychological disorders, and affirmed that no psychologist should ever participate in "therapy" designed to change the sexual orientation of a patient.

The genetic basis of homosexuality has obvious implications for the political debate. If genetic, then homosexuality is natural and deserving of acceptance. This should stop Christian condemnation of gay people, for it would be inconsistent to condemn what God has made. It also makes inconsistent their arguments that they "hate the homosexuality but love the homosexual." In this case, the behavior is embedded in the very genes of the individual, making the two inseparable. It's time Christian conservatives accepted the fact the Bible's laws against homosexuality, like its laws permitting slavery, monarchy, and genocide, are archaic and no longer applicable to the current age.

"This 'born gay' idea is not new, not proven, and frequently contradicted by what the researchers actually said."

A BIOLOGICAL BASIS FOR HOMOSEXUALITY HAS NOT BEEN PROVEN

Steve Calverley and Rob Goetze

There has been no conclusive evidence proving that homosexuality is biologically determined, argue Steve Calverley and Rob Goetze in the following viewpoint. The lack of control groups or random population samples are flaws that discredit the three most widely cited scientific studies, the authors assert. Moreover, Calverley and Goetze point out, ensuing research has failed to verify—and has sometimes contradicted—the alleged link between genetics and homosexuality. Calverley facilitates support groups for New Direction for Life Ministries of Canada, a Christian organization for homosexuals who wish to change their sexual orientation. Goetze is the director of the Toronto-based New Direction for Life Ministries of Canada.

As you read, consider the following questions:

1. According to Calverley and Goetze, what was a major flaw in Simon LeVay's study measuring the INAH-3 area of the brain?
2. According to the authors, what evidence from the study conducted by Michael Bailey and Richard Pillard suggests that homosexuality is caused by environmental factors?
3. How did Bailey and Pillard recruit subjects for their study, according to the authors?

Reprinted from Steve Calverley and Rob Goetze, "Are People 'Born Gay'? A Look at the Most Cited Biological Research Studies," web article at www.execulink.com/~newdirec/2_biol.htm, September 22, 1998. Reprinted by permission of the authors and New Direction for Life Ministries.

"**B**orn gay." The idea that homosexuality is genetic, or at least biologically predetermined and unchangeable, has received a great amount of media coverage presenting it as "new scientific fact." What is often not known is that this "born gay" idea is not new, not proven, and frequently contradicted by what the researchers actually said. At least as far back as 1899, German researcher Magnus Hirschfeld regarded homosexuality as congenital—meaning, "born that way"—and he asked for legal equality based on this thinking.

Now, a century later, the idea that homosexual persons are born that way has again received a great amount of media attention. As new research studies were published, the popular press presented these as evidence that people are "born gay" and that sexual orientation is therefore unchangeable. What has been quietly happening, though, is that the "science" behind this idea is falling apart. Here we briefly examine the three most cited studies, from Simon LeVay, Michael Bailey & Richard Pillard, and Dean Hamer:

SIMON LEVAY AND BRAIN STRUCTURE

"Time and again I have been described as someone who 'proved that homosexuality is genetic'. . . I did not."

Simon LeVay in *The Sexual Brain*, p. 122.

Simon LeVay, a neuroscientist, studied the brains from 41 corpses, including 6 women, 19 homosexual men, and 16 men presumed to be heterosexual. A small area of the brain, the INAH-3, was similar in size in women and homosexual men, but larger in heterosexual men. He suggested that this might be evidence for an actual structural difference in the brains of gay men. There are, however, numerous problems:

• In comparing the size of the INAH-3, he presumed that the 16 "heterosexual" men were, in fact, heterosexual. Only two of them had denied homosexual activities; for the rest, sexual histories were not available. Thus, he was actually comparing homosexual men with men of unknown sexual orientation! This, obviously, is a major flaw in scientific method.

• The volume of the INAH-3 may not be a relevant measure:

— Scientists disagree on the most accurate way to measure the INAH-3. LeVay measured the volume; other scientists claim it is more accurate to measure the actual number of neurons. Clarifying the potential problem, some have suggested that using a volume method to project impact on sexual orientation may be like trying to determine intelligence by a person's hat size.

— When different laboratories have measured the four areas of the INAH (including INAH-3), their results conflicted. For example, Dick Swaab et al (1985) found that the INAH-1 was larger in men, while LeVay (1991) found no difference between men and women. Laura Allen et al (1989) found the INAH-2 to be larger in men than in some women, while LeVay (1991) again found no difference.

• The above problems aside, even the data from LeVay's study did not prove that anyone was born gay. This is the case for at least two reasons:

— Both groups of men covered essentially the same range of sizes. One could be gay with a small INAH-3 or with a large one. One could also be in the "heterosexual" category with either a small or large INAH-3. Clearly, these men were not held to a sexual orientation by their INAH-3 biology! As the data shows, the INAH-3 size of three of the homosexual men puts them clearly in the "heterosexual" category (with one having the second largest INAH-3!). If all you know about any of LeVay's subjects is INAH-3 size, you could not accurately predict whether they are heterosexual or homosexual, male or female.

— A study that showed a clear difference in INAH-3 sizes would still leave another question unanswered: are men gay because of a smaller INAH-3, or was their INAH-3 smaller because of their homosexual actions, thoughts, and/or feelings? It is known that the brain does change in response to changes in behaviour and environment. For example, the February 24, 1992, Newsweek reported that "in people reading Braille after becoming blind, the area of the brain controlling the reading finger grew larger." As well, in male songbirds, "the brain area associated with mating is not only larger than in the female, but varies according to the season."

TWINS AND OTHER BROTHERS

Bailey and Pillard studied pairs of brothers—identical twins, non-identical twins, other biological brothers, and adoptive brothers—where at least one was gay. At first glance, their findings looked like a pattern for homosexuality being genetically influenced. Identical twins were both homosexual 52% of the time; non-identical twins, 22%; other biological brothers, 9.2%; and adoptive brothers, 10.5%. A closer look reveals significant problems with a "born gay" conclusion to this study:

TABLE I

	Shared genes (overall):	Both homosexual: Expectation if genetic:	Results from B&P study:
Identical brothers	100%	100%	52%
Non-identical brothers	50%	50%	22%
Other biological brothers	50%	50%	9%
Adoptive brothers	0%	1–4%	11%

Steve Calverley and Rob Goetze, on-line report, 1998.

• "In order for such a study to be meaningful, you'd have to look at twins raised apart," says Anne Fausto Sterling, a biologist. The brothers in this study were raised together in their families.

• All the results were different from what one would expect if homosexuality was directly genetic:

— Because identical twin brothers share 100% of their genes overall, we would expect that if one was homosexual, the other would also be homosexual, 100% of the time. Instead, this study found that they were both homosexual only 52% of the time.

— Although completely unrelated genetically, adoptive brothers were more likely to both be gay than the biological brothers, who share half their genes! This piece of data prompted the December 24, 1993, issue of the journal *Science* to respond: "this . . . suggests that there is no genetic component, but rather an environmental component shared in families."

— If homosexuality were genetic, one would expect each number in the column "Results from B&P study" in Table I to be identical to the corresponding number in the "Expectation if genetic" column. Each one is significantly different!

• Finally, Bailey & Pillard did not use a random sample. The men in the study were recruited through advertisements in gay newspapers and magazines.

DEAN HAMER AND GENETIC MARKERS

Hamer studied 40 pairs of homosexual brothers, and reported that 33 pairs shared a set of five genetic markers. Reporting the story, the July 26, 1993, *Time* magazine's cover read "BORN GAY Science Finds a Genetic Link." Hamer, however, was more cautious. He felt that it played "some role" in a minority of 5 to 30% of gay men. This is a rather distant reality from finding the "gay gene" and it left two critical questions: just how much influence was "some role" thought to be, and what about the other 70 to 95%?

- Based on a simple genetic theory, one would expect 50%, or 20 pairs, to have the same markers. Why did 7 pairs of gay brothers not share a set of genetic markers?

- Hamer did not check to see if the heterosexual brothers of the homosexual men also had such a genetic marker. Thus, there was no control group in this study. Here too, this obviously is a major flaw in scientific method.

- Since that time, Science has reported that George Ebers, a researcher at the University of Western Ontario, has attempted to duplicate the study but found "no evidence, not even a trend," for the "genetic link." In the scientific world, that is a big problem.

Now even the gay and pro-gay press are acknowledging the problems. In her 1996 book, Gender Shock, writer and lesbian person Phyllis Burke, quoting Dr. Paul Billings, an internist and human geneticist, calls the born gay idea "a new fish story." A gay publication, The Guide, writes Hamer's story under the title "Gene Scam?"

Born gay? Ironically, what the studies actually suggest is that persons who experience same-sex attraction are not prisoners of their biology. That's good news for same-gender-attracted people who would rather pursue other options.

> "For the vast majority of humans, [sexual] orientation develops autonomously, largely independent of environmental circumstances, and is almost impervious to change."

THE CAUSES OF HOMOSEXUALITY ARE PROBABLY GENETIC

Richard Pillard

A homosexual orientation is most likely the result of genetics, argues Richard Pillard in the following viewpoint. Although a specific "gay gene" has not yet been identified, surveys of families, siblings, and twins reveal that gays and lesbians have a significantly higher percentage of homosexual blood relatives than do heterosexuals, Pillard contends. Furthermore, the existence of several pairs of gay male identical twins who were raised separately strongly suggests that homosexuality is an inherited trait and not the result of environmental factors, the author maintains. Pillard is a professor of psychiatry at the Boston University School of Medicine.

As you read, consider the following questions:

1. According to Pillard, what anthropological evidence suggests that sexual orientation is not affected by conditioning?
2. Why are behavior traits difficult to analyze genetically, according to the author?
3. What is "kin altruism," according to Pillard?

Abridged from Richard Pillard, "The Genetic Theory of Sexual Orientation," *The Harvard Gay and Lesbian Review*, Winter 1997. Reprinted with permission.

My medical school textbook of psychiatry, now more than 30 years old, discussed homosexuality in a section sandwiched between "inadequate and infantile behavior" and "sexual intercourse with domestic animals." Within one professional lifetime, the scientific study of sexual orientation has left the ghetto of psychopathology and moved to the gentrified neighborhood of mainstream culture. Perhaps the celebrity status of gay and lesbian studies is not so surprising when we reflect that what steers some people toward being straight is as little understood as what leads others to be gay. Everyone is curious about the origin of his or her desires, why we are attracted to men or to women, to a hairy partner or a smooth one, to someone blond, brunette, or (as some of us hope) bald. The precise delineation of human lusts remains, strange to say, relatively unknown territory.

EXAMINING THE ROOTS OF SEXUAL DESIRE

Members of my profession have, to be sure, described the more obscure sexual desires. My favorite case vignettes come from psychiatrist and jurist Richard von Krafft-Ebing (1840–1902). In his famous *Psychopathia Sexualis*, Krafft-Ebing described several hundred individuals referred for forensic evaluation. There is, for example, the young man who, in the dark of night, dug open the graves of the freshly dead and with his bare hands clawed open their coffins "in nowise sensible in his excitement to the injuries he thus inflicted on himself." I will spare the reader further details, which the author has discreetly rendered in Latin.

On a more mundane line, Krafft-Ebing wrote of a man attracted to women who limp, and remarked that, as a youth, this man had a nurse with a lame leg. He speculated that "in the life of every fetishist, some partial sexual impression occurs with the first awakening of the *vita sexualis*." Here, I think Krafft-Ebing was on to something. First attractions probably have unusual power to fixate the libido, particularly if combined with some degree of anxiety. The more modern ideas of imprinting and instrumental conditioning come to mind. Pair an unconditionally pleasant stimulus such as genital fondling with a neutral stimulus like the feel and smell of undershorts in the process of removal and you can make a reasonable case for the popularity of Calvin Klein.

I have to admit, however, that when it comes to being gay or straight, environmental explanations—learning, conditioning, imprinting, and so on—fail to strike me as deeply convincing. It may indeed be that as infants all of us were pleasured and intimidated in ways that shaped our adult sexual orientation. Parental influences account for a lot, but my vote is that sexual orientation comes from a different place. Wherever that place is, it must originate in the earliest years of life if not prenatally, because most lesbians and gay men are marked as such early in childhood by virtue of their play behavior, which tends so often to be gender-atypical. The sissy boy and the tomboy girl may be stereotypes, but they are also powerful predictors of adult sexual orientation.

A REBUTTAL TO ENVIRONMENTAL EXPLANATIONS

A more serious rebuttal to simple learning explanations comes from the work of anthropologist Gilbert Herdt. Herdt studied the Sambia tribe in New Guinea and their mythology of masculine development. A Sambia boy must imbibe quantities of semen in order to become virile and able to ejaculate semen himself. Thus, the pre-adolescent boys fellate older adolescent and young adult men to fill their bodies with the masculinizing fluid. Later, they will be fellated in their turn by the younger initiates. It works for the Sambia. Since Sambian youth are having homosexual orgasms year after year, taking first one part and eventually the other and having a perfectly enjoyable time, why don't they become "conditioned" to same-sex arousal and continue to seek it after their time comes to leave the men's hut, to court and marry? They just don't. The occasional older man does want to keep doing it with guys (it's a small tribe) but he is the rare exception.

I want to advance a different theory, simple and rather general: sexual orientation resides in the deep structure of human personality. It is wired into our brains. For the vast majority of humans, an orientation develops autonomously, largely independent of environmental circumstances, and is almost impervious to change. Even people with quite atypical brains, schizophrenics and the mentally retarded, almost always have a sense of being either gay or straight.

If sexual orientation is indeed wired in, is it so wired genetically, or is it due to some accidental influence in the early environment, inside or outside the womb? An example of a prenatal influence is the increase of schizophrenia in the offspring of Dutch mothers pregnant during the great famine winter at the end of World War II. Presumably, the lack of a particular amino acid in the mother's diet affected the developing brain of the offspring. In the same vein, German endocrinologist Günter Dörner

29

suggested that more gay men are born to mothers who experience prenatal stress. Dörner's argument is hard to prove or disprove. One woman's stress is another's exciting challenge; however, on balance, the maternal stress theory lacks convincing data.

TESTING GENETIC THEORIES

That sexual orientation is genetically endowed is hardly a new idea. The great sexologists of the past, including Sigmund Freud, Magnus Hirschfeld, Havelock Ellis, and others, have all accepted it as probable. One way to test whether genes influence sexual orientation is to see if it is familial. Should being lesbian or gay turn out to be familial, the genetic theory gets a boost—though of course traits run in families for other than genetic reasons. On the other hand, if orientation is not familial, the genetic hypothesis dies. Some years ago, I thought it would be worthwhile to make a careful study of this issue. I was aware of families that had lots of gay kin, and as I reviewed the literature, there seemed to be certain families that were gay-loaded, the French Bourbon monarchy for one.

Our team at Boston University recruited as random a sample as we could find of men and women willing to provide a sexual history. We then located as many of their siblings as we could coax to join the study. Of the heterosexual men, about four percent had brothers exclusively or predominately gay. This was reassuring because four percent is close to the national average for men with a lifelong history of same-sex attraction, suggesting that our sampling and interviewing techniques were working properly. The picture was very different for the gay male subjects. They had five times as many gay brothers as the straight men, over 20 percent altogether. Any reader of this article can do a low-tech replication. Ask a random sample of the gay men you know how many brothers they have and then how many of those brothers are gay. Average the results from as few as 20 respondents and you will become a believer. The lesbians we interviewed also had more lesbian sisters than the heterosexual women, although the difference wasn't as large. Some families had both gay brothers and lesbian sisters and some had interesting patterns of gayness in their more distant relatives.

STUDIES OF TWINS

Shortly thereafter, we participated in a study begun by psychologist Michael Bailey at Northwestern University. Bailey gathered a group of gay twins, some identical and some fraternal, and then ascertained the orientation of the co-twin. A genetic hypothesis predicts that the identical twins will be concordant (both gay) in the 50 to 70 percent range, while the fraternal twins will both be gay only as often as the gay brother pairs in the family study, about 20 percent. Adding a sample of adopted siblings of gay probands is an important control; the adoptees should be gay no more often than the general population, about two percent for women, four percent for men. This was indeed the approximate result obtained from several large samples.

GENETIC FACTORS

A 1991 study by Michael Bailey and Richard Pillard investigated the sexual orientation of the siblings of 110 gay men. These researchers found a concordance rate of 52 percent for identical (monozygotic, or MZ) twins, 22 percent for fraternal (dizygotic, or DZ) twins, 9 percent for nontwin brothers, and 11 percent for adopted brothers. In a similar 1993 study with lesbians and bisexual women, Bailey and his colleagues reported a concordance rate of 48 percent for MZ twins, 16 percent for DZ twins, 14 percent for nontwin sisters, and 6 percent for adoptive sisters. These findings suggest that there may be a genetic component to homosexual orientation (although they do not speak directly to heterosexuality). The concordance rate increases as the degree of genetic similarity increases, as would be expected from a genetic hypothesis.

Janis S. Bohan, *Psychology and Sexual Orientation*, 1996.

Twins and siblings can be alike for other than genetic reasons. It is commonly supposed that sexual orientation is shaped to some extent by family influences that are naturally more alike for identical twins. To our surprise, the heritability calculations revealed that the most powerful environmental influences were not those that the twins shared but those they did not share. In other words, insofar as life circumstances contribute to sexual orientation, it isn't having the same mother and father, living in the same house, getting beaten up by the same bully that matters, but instead the different experiences twins might have (e.g., one takes piano lessons, the other becomes a Boy Scout)—although what those different experiences might be, this research design could not identify. The problem is that nobody knows what's relevant to the development of sexual orientation. It may be true, for example, that gay boys have distant fathers and protective mothers, but what is the cause-effect relationship here?

One powerful way to get an idea of the relative contribution of nature and nurture is to look at identical twins, one of whom is gay, who have been separated shortly after birth and raised in separate environments. They are rare persons, of course, and only a few have been reported in the medical literature. Among the four known women pairs, none were concordant for being lesbian, but among the men, several pairs were both gay. Moreover, the concordant twins, beside being gay, tended to share other aspects of their personality, including their particular sexual tastes. Taken as a whole, the family and twin data strongly suggest a genetic influence on sexuality, though perhaps a stronger one in men than in women.

HEREDITY PLAYS AN IMPORTANT ROLE

It might seem that heredity can be only part of the story because, if genes were everything, the identical twin pairs, however they were raised, should *always* be concordant—assuming they have an identical genetic endowment. However, recent genome research shows that identical twins in fact acquire some interesting differences. This happens because after the fertilized egg separates into two individuals, there is a period of genomic instability during which subtle changes occur in the DNA sequencing of the two, now separate, fetuses. Whether these changes have anything to do with personality, much less with sexual orientation, is not known, but this opens the possibility that heredity may play an even more important role in determining how we behave than the classical twin studies have led us to assume.

The ultimate test of a genetic basis for a behavioral trait is of course to find the gene or genes and discover what they do. This will not be easy, judging from what we know about genes. The search for the gene for Huntington's Disease serves as a caution against optimism. Huntington's is a stereotyped neurologic disorder, easy to diagnose, and transmitted as an autosomal dominant with complete penetrance. The Huntington's gene ought to be easy to find, but it took ten years and tens of millions of dollars to locate and sequence it. We now know that Huntington's Disease is caused by one gene of large effect, but we assume that the genes influencing behavior act in a chorus, each contributing only a small part. Moreover, the expression of some genes depends on the presence of specific genes elsewhere in the genome, or on an environmental trigger that amplifies or damps a gene's potential. One imagines, therefore, that the genetic analysis of complex behavior traits will be extremely difficult. The path from gene product (a protein structure or enzyme) to the eventual behavior remains a black box. Still, molecular biology is perhaps the most rapidly advancing science within medicine, so it is likely that the genetic analysis of "normal" behaviors is going to move ahead very quickly. . . .

WHY DOES HOMOSEXUALITY PERSIST?

The discussion so far still leaves bare the question why an orientation that appears so inimical to reproduction might nevertheless persist in human or animal populations. Homosexuality needs to demonstrate a survival benefit sufficient to offset the reproductive cost that the orientation would be expected to exact. Most reproductively disadvantageous traits occur because of occasional and random mutations which are gradually selected out of the kindred. Huntington's Disease, for example, occurs in only about four people per million. The gay/lesbian phenotype is far too common to be entirely the result of deleterious mutations. If genetic, it must have undergone some degree of favorable selection. One concept to understand about "reproductive success" is that it can be realized by different strategies. The oak produces thousands of acorns and is lucky if one or two grow to make acorns of their own. The larger land mammals, on the other hand, have relatively few offspring and are metabolically expensive to bear. A successful strategy for big creatures like ourselves is to invest heavily in guarding and protecting the relatively few offspring that we are able to have.

This line of thinking, elaborated by biologists Robert Trivers and James Weinrich, among others, is that gay people may have evolved character traits of an altruistic nature that prompt them to work harder for the protection and advancement of closely related family members rather than invest in having children of their own. This idea, called "kin altruism," results from the simple calculus that two nephews or nieces are genetically equivalent to one son or daughter. Reproductive sacrifice explainable by a theory of kin altruism has been demonstrated in some animal species but remains speculative for humans, most of whom, sad to say, seem rather short in the department of altruism.

Ray Blanchard and his colleagues at the Clarke Institute in Toronto recently analyzed thousands of families and found that gay men have a later birth order than straight. Specifically, the gay men had more older brothers but not more older sisters once the older brothers were taken into account. A psychodevelopmental explanation springs to mind: a young boy might develop homosexual attractions more readily if an older brother is in the picture. But a biological explanation is also on the horizon. The placenta supporting every human pregnancy has small protein fingers that engage the mother's bloodstream by digging into the wall of her uterus. When the placenta is shed, some of the placental cells remain in the uterine wall and can be demonstrated to be alive and well years later. These cells came from the fetus and contain its genome. Is it possible that some cells of an early pregnancy remain behind and, by an unexplained mechanism, try to capture the resources of subsequent pregnancies, a sort of biological primogeniture? I like this odd (and admittedly remote) possibility because it shows how much is still unexpected in the biology of human sexuality.

Behavior genetics applied to sexual orientation encounters a variety of criticisms. In this debate, I feel like a detective who's presenting his case to the district attorney. I have scraps and clues, hypotheses that sometimes hang together but that also have gaps. But the DA must be a skeptic. He has to put my case before a jury whom he must convince beyond a reasonable doubt. The standard of proof rises as the investigation proceeds. (Thanks to Jim Weinrich for the analogy.) The most I can say is that no one has yet put forward evidence that is devastating to my case.

There is one criticism I want at least to touch on, namely that genetic theories pander to homophobia. If "gay genes" are discovered, how much easier will it be to eradicate them. Opinion surveys are unanimous that people who endorse a genetic hypothesis are more sympathetic to lesbians and gays than people who hold to a purely environmental theory. Still, technology has a way of biting back. No scientific knowledge is risk-free, and this must surely include genetic investigations of sexual orientation. One might take a sort of reverse comfort in knowing that homophobia, like racism (and all the xenophobias), exists regardless of whatever might be considered "the facts" of the moment. Research on human sexuality will, by its nature, evoke resistance and fear, to some extent legitimately. Here is where I think social science research has a valuable role. There ought to be funded research programs not only to unravel the genome but to unravel the ethical and psychological dilemmas that accompany the new insights that behavior genetics will generate.

Scientific research is permeated by values. Mine are that it is better to know something than not to know it. I believe that same-sex desire will remain a topic of interest and study for a long time. I'm confident that biological knowledge will prove it to be a valuable trait, selected by evolution precisely because it contributes some quality that was useful, perhaps even essential, to the sudden ascendancy of human beings among all the primates.

"Evidence contradicts the notion that homosexuality is genetic destiny and points primarily toward environmental and emotional problems."

THE CAUSES OF HOMOSEXUALITY ARE PROBABLY ENVIRONMENTAL

Part I: Illinois Family Institute, Part II: Cal Thomas

The authors of the following two-part viewpoint claim that homosexuality is typically caused by environmental—not biological or genetic—factors. In Part I, the Illinois Family Institute, a research and advocacy organization that supports traditional Judeo-Christian values, contends that homosexuality is often the result of emotionally damaging parent-child relationships. With the help of therapy, homosexuals can become heterosexual, the institute maintains. In Part II, syndicated columnist Cal Thomas argues that homosexuality is a learned response to traumatic childhood experiences. Those who deny that therapy can help homosexuals change their orientation are motivated by a "gay rights" political agenda, Thomas asserts.

As you read, consider the following questions:
1. According to the Illinois Family Institute, what percentage of Americans believe that homosexual acts are wrong?
2. What evidence contradicts the 1991 study that concluded that homosexuality is the result of genetics, according to the institute?
3. According to Thomas, what percentage of surveyed homosexuals became exclusively heterosexual after undergoing reparative therapy?

Part I: Excerpted from the Illinois Family Institute's "Summary Statement on Homosexuality," at www.ilfaminst.com/homopb.htm, 1997. Reprinted with permission. Part II: Reprinted from Cal Thomas, "Gay Conversion: A Reality Psychologists Ignore," Christian American, January/February 1998, by permission of the Los Angeles Times Syndicate; © 1998 Los Angeles Times.

I

Evidence contradicts the notion that homosexuality is genetic destiny and points primarily toward environmental and emotional problems, most often stemming from poor childhood relationships with same-sex parents. Moreover, therapeutic efforts to help people move from homosexuality to heterosexuality are frequently successful.

In light of these origins, it is clear that homosexuality is not a healthy state. Indeed, homosexuals typically are heavily involved with numerous destructive behaviors—from extreme promiscuity to substance abuse to the spreading of numerous diseases—that damage both themselves and the society around them.

PUBLIC POLICY IMPLICATIONS

Thus, homosexuality is not inevitable; not incurable; and not to be encouraged. Public policy implications include the following:

• "Gay rights" laws are measures to normalize homosexuality, seeking to place it on a par with (say) race as something that cannot and should not change. They do not secure "civil rights" (no "gay rights" laws are needed to provide the rights of all citizens—e.g., trial by jury). Rather, they wage cultural aggression against people who morally oppose homosexuality, and violate the consciences of those individuals. (Consider, e.g., a case where a landlord is ordered to rent an apartment he has reason to believe will be used for homosexual acts.)

• Public schools should not subvert the deeply-held values of a large number of the taxpayers. Fully 66 percent of Americans believe homosexual acts are "always wrong." The state should not fund schools and community colleges which promote homosexual practices, equate homosexual behavior to heterosexual behavior, or equate sexual orientation to race or ethnicity.

• Adoption by two persons of the same sex should not be permitted. Activist judges have ruled in favor of this, citing the lack of an explicit legal prohibition on the practice. As a remedy, the law should clearly affirm that homosexual adoption is outside the intent of the legislature. Likewise, marriage should be clearly defined in law as an institution between persons of opposite gender, in accordance with the longstanding understanding of our culture, and as a safeguard against judicial activism.

• Sound social policy will uphold the heterosexual, marriage-based, two-parent family as its foundation, and as the setting in which sexuality may truly and rightly be realized. It must not degrade marriage and family by seeking to artificially elevate "alternative lifestyles" to the same level. It will reject homosexual acts while helping people tempted to those acts to overcome them and move into a healthy lifestyle. . . .

THE CAUSES OF HOMOSEXUALITY

It is argued that homosexuality is caused by genetic factors alone, and thus that it is natural, normal, and healthy. We, however, argue that it is neither inevitable nor unchangeable; that it is socially, medically, and morally unhealthy; and therefore that government should not legitimize homosexuality, but uphold the family unit—the foundation of a good society.

It is often claimed that homosexuals are simply "born that way." Yet even studies that have been used to argue that point have shown otherwise. For example: in 1991, a widely-publicized study conducted by Michael Bailey and Richard Pillard found that half the identical twin brothers of homosexual men were themselves homosexual. This conclusion was seized upon by gay activists as proof that homosexuality is solely a matter of biological destiny. But if that were the case, the number should not have been half; all the brothers should have been homosexual. As it is, other research has reported far less than half among identical twins—10 percent, according to a British study conducted by M. King and E. McDonald. (Even that number may be high; both studies drew their subjects from readers of homosexual periodicals, who may not be representative.)

Other problems emerged in the 1991 study. For example, critics pointed out, 22 percent of fraternal (i.e., non-identical) twin brothers of homosexual men were found to be homosexual. Yet among non-twin brothers, the rate was less than half that—9.2 percent. Since fraternal twins share no genetic material, there was no genetic reason that they should be more likely to share a brother's sexual orientation than were non-twins. It is also odd that even the non-twin brothers should be homosexual at a rate so much higher than the general populace, where the overall rate is today commonly accepted to be between 1 and 3 percent.

On the other hand, this difference is consistent with the understanding that life experiences play a major role in homosexuality. It stands to reason that children who grow up together will be exposed to similar influences, and may react in similar ways. It also follows that this trend will be especially apparent among twins, who grow up not just in the same setting but at the same time. Moreover, it is known that the experiences of twins are often unusual and sometimes psychologically damaging. (For example, the aforementioned British study found that identical twins have an unusually high rate of incestuous relationships with each other.)

Space does not permit a detailed analysis of research on the causes of homosexuality. The important point is that attempts to reduce them to the merely physical are, at best, radical oversimplifications. As Columbia University research psychiatrists William Byne and Bruce Parsons state, "the appeal of current biologic explanations for sexual orientation may derive more from dissatisfaction with the present status of psychosocial explanations than from a substantial body of experimental data. Critical review shows the evidence favoring a biologic theory to be lacking."

EMOTIONAL DAMAGE IS A PRIMARY FACTOR

Biology may play some role in some cases, but it is far from universally decisive. Considerable evidence, however, suggests that emotional damage, typically sustained in childhood, may be the principal driving factor behind homosexuality.

Male homosexuals tend to have had "distant, hostile, or rejecting childhood relationships" with their fathers, with the result that the sons develop what Dr. Elizabeth Moberly describes as a "defensive detachment" leading to "same-sex ambivalence." Unable to identify with his father's masculinity, the son will detach from not only the father but masculinity itself; yet at the same time he seeks to heal the breach and make contact with masculinity. As one man put it, "Even before I came [to therapy], I realized that I did not want another man—I wanted a manly me."

HOMOSEXUALS CAN CHANGE

Yes, it is possible for a wrongdoer to change. The Scriptures acknowledge this by encouraging people to strip off the old personality and put on the new one and to "be made new in the force actuating the mind." (Ephesians 4:22-24) Those who practice what is bad, including homosexuals, can make radical changes in their pattern of thinking and behavior, and many have indeed been successful in making this transformation. Jesus himself preached to such ones; and on showing repentance, they became acceptable to him.—Matthew 21:31,32. . . .

Christians are ready to offer the needed spiritual support, even to those who are still struggling with homosexual inclinations. This is in harmony with God's own manifestation of love, for the Bible says: "God recommends his own love to us in that, while we were yet sinners, Christ died for us."—Romans 5:8.

Awake! December 8, 1997.

Lesbians, likewise, tend to have had early detachments from their mothers which they desire to heal. "The most common activities of homosexual women consist mainly of the mutual playing of mother and child," notes University of Washington psychiatrist Theo L. Dorpat. Some see their mothers as weak, pathetic, vulnerable, or otherwise inadequate; they may identify with their fathers, whom they see as strong and safe.

In such cases, a girl's sense of her own femininity is stunted. In still other cases, lesbianism results from sexual abuse and a consequent fear of male sexuality.

But the desire to gain love or a basic sense of self cannot be secured by sex. Indeed, that desire is perverted by its sexualization. "Erotic ecstasy will never heal emotional trauma," notes [researcher] Larry Burtoft. "A thousand orgasms cannot create a sense of self, unless it is a false self, a half-person, a perpetual question mark."

HOMOSEXUALITY CAN BE TREATED

It must be noted that homosexuality can be treated and, at least in many cases, cured. Homosexual activists vehemently deny this, doubtless because they resent the idea that there is anything about them that needs curing. But it is an undeniable fact; somewhere between 30 and 70 percent of homosexuals who undergo psychiatric therapy successfully turn away from homosexuality and adopt heterosexual lifestyles. This is not to say that all homosexuals can change their inclinations (though we do not know they cannot, and we do know that all may control their behavior). It is to say that any blanket statement that people afflicted with homosexual temptations cannot change is demonstrably false. . . .

Because homosexuality is not decreed by nature, it follows that society's attitude can have an effect on it. To be sure, it cannot be prevented or cured by social disapproval alone. But such disapproval—that is, a recognition that homosexuality is harmful and destructive—is a necessary prerequisite. . . .

For the most part, social attitudes toward homosexuality will be determined outside the legislative arena. That is as it should be.

Our position can be summarized as loving the sinner while hating the sin. Contrary to the hysterical screams of activists who charge that opposing homosexuality is tantamount to "hate," this position is perfectly consistent. Opponents of drug abuse frequently show zero tolerance for the behavior they oppose, yet they are never accused of "hating" abusers. Indeed, the anti-drug movement consists largely of parents, siblings, and friends motivated by love.

So it is here. Precisely because we do care, we cannot simply look the other way or ask homosexuals to remain in the closet. We must seek to help them out of their self-destructive lifestyles. As columnist Joseph Sobran puts it, "homosexuals should be encouraged to realize that homosexuality is not worthy of them."

II

The American Psychological Association (APA) has adopted a resolution it hopes will limit treatment designed to change the behavior of homosexual men and women. Known as "reparative therapy," the technique seeks to help homosexuals troubled by their lives.

What's wrong with that, you might ask, so long as people are not coerced or intimidated?

From the gay rights lobby's point of view, there is plenty wrong.

If homosexuals can change their behavior, then their argument for special protection under civil rights laws designed for people whose status has nothing to do with behavior (i.e., racial minorities, women, the disabled) falls apart. That's why they have stepped up the media assault, including 30 gay and lesbian characters showing up on television in the 1998 season, according to the Gay and Lesbian Alliance Against Defamation. It is also why they conduct organized letter-writing campaigns to newspapers demanding the censoring of any writer who does not embrace and promote their view.

The APA backed away from wording that would have deemed reparative therapy "unethical," but it's only a matter of time before such a resolution is approved, given the political direction of the organization. It has an office dedicated exclusively to gay, lesbian and bisexual issues that helped craft the approved resolution.

HOMOSEXUALITY IS NOT INHERITED

But the facts (as opposed to the politics) are that people who want to change *can* change, because it is behavior at issue—not race, gender or physical abilities.

In 1980, clinical psychologist Dr. Robert Kronemeyer wrote in his book *Overcoming Homosexuality*: "With rare exceptions, homosexuality is neither inherited nor the result of some glandular disturbance or the scrambling of genes or chromosomes.

Homosexuals are made, not born 'that way.' Buried under the 'gay' exterior of the homosexual is the hurt and rage that crippled his or her capacity for true maturation, for healthy growth and love. After a quarter-century of clinical experience, I firmly believe that homosexuality is a learned response to early painful experiences and that it can be unlearned.

For those homosexuals who are unhappy with their lives and can find effective therapy, it can be overcome."

There's no "hate or bigotry" (as gay rights people brand those who disagree with them) in that statement. Just clinical, observable facts.

OVERCOMING HOMOSEXUALITY

One of the most successful at reparative therapy is the National Association for Research and Therapy of Homosexuality (NARTH). In May 1997, NARTH released the results of a two-year study conducted among nearly 860 individuals struggling to overcome homosexuality and more than 200 psychologists and therapists who treat them.

The survey found that before treatment 68 percent of respondents perceived themselves as exclusively or almost entirely homosexual, with another 22 percent stating they were more homosexual than heterosexual.

After treatment, only 13 percent perceived themselves as exclusively or almost entirely homosexual, while 33 percent described themselves as either exclusively or almost entirely heterosexual.

Ninety-nine percent said they believe treatment to change homosexuality can be effective and valuable.

Even their thought-life had been transformed, with 63 percent indicating they had frequent and intense homosexual thoughts before treatment and only 3 percent indicating they had such thoughts after treatment. Among the psychotherapists, 82 percent said they believe therapy can help change unwanted homosexuality.

A POLITICAL AGENDA

Why would a professional association like APA oppose therapy for people who say they want to change their lifestyles and thoughts?

How is medicine or science advanced when an organization denies homosexuals the freedom to choose (something virtually all professional medical societies support when it comes to abortion)?

Why would the APA oppose treatment that is not coercive and that is conducted only with those who seek it unless it has a political agenda?

| "Mating behavior in humans may be more about the interaction among genes, biological processes, and cognitive influences than it is about genes alone."

A Variety of Factors May Cause Homosexuality

Charles Lopresto

In the following viewpoint, Charles Lopresto contends that homosexuality most likely results from a combination of genetic, biological, and environmental factors. He asserts that human sexual behavior is highly variable because it is determined by ancient genes, brain function, biological processes, and cognitive influences such as social and cultural attitudes. For example, Lopresto points out, gay, bisexual, or heterosexual individuals could have a mild genetic inclination toward homosexuality that is modified in various ways by prenatal hormonal influences, parental conditioning, childhood experiences, and societal opinion. Lopresto is an associate professor of psychology at Loyola College in Baltimore, Maryland.

As you read, consider the following questions:
1. What is the difference between a genotype and a phenotype, according to Lopresto?
2. According to this viewpoint, what is an allele?
3. If sexual orientation is a one-gene trait, which alleles would result in a bisexual genotype, according to Lopresto?

Reprinted from Charles Lopresto's guest column as originally published on The Gay Gene website at http://members.aol.com/gaygene, edited by Chandler Burr, by permission of the author, who wishes the reader to know that this is a work in progress.

B efore beginning, I think it important to underscore a clarifi-cation that genetic researchers have made repeatedly—that is, sexuality and sexual orientation are two different things. For the sake of this viewpoint, I'm defining sexual orientation as the gender one finds sexually and romantically attractive, i.e., a di-rectional responsivity of sorts. Sexuality, on the other hand, deals with the totality of cognitive, affective and behavioral ex-pressions of one's sexual self, a totality which unquestionably involves complex interactions of biology and environment.

GENES DO NOT ALWAYS DETERMINE OUTCOMES

A review of current literature provides a compelling body of re-search linking sexual orientation to genes. But I'd like to play devil's advocate here. A truly scientific approach to the topic de-mands a critical appraisal of the data, right? Let me start out by arguing in favor of the existence of genes that control sexual orientation in people—and then argue later that these genes sometimes don't determine outcomes. Start with the fact that as you go higher up through the phylogenic scale, from simpler organisms to more complex ones, genes have less and less influ-ence on sexual behavior. Let me illustrate.

Obviously, in lower, simpler organisms genes significantly regulate and limit mating behavior to certain times of the month or season—fruit flies are clearly strictly programmed as to when and how they mate. Humans on the other hand are ca-pable of mating at any time. But given that we humans evolved from simpler organisms, it is highly probable that genes deter-mining mating behavior have not yet been eradicated from our genetic maps ("genotypes"). These ancient genes still sit inside us in a sort of dormant state, no longer "functional" or ex-pressed in our behavior (our "phenotype"), since instead of be-ing sexually predictable like lower organisms, we clearly display tremendous variability in mating behavior. Why is this?

It's pretty clear that human sexual behavior—along with its genetic origins—is strongly influenced by non-genetic biologi-cal processes and, ultimately, by the cerebral cortex. In the case of mating behavior, despite the fact that we might have a genetic "push" from mating gene(s), our behavior comes both from that push and from intervening biological and cognitive vari-ables (e.g., fatigue, stress, attitudes, etc.). In the final analysis, then, mating behavior in humans may be more about the inter-action among genes, biological processes, and cognitive influ-ences than it is about genes alone. And therein lies my bias in this scientific debate. Even if a gay gene (or genes) is found, can we assume, given the propensity of data suggesting the complexity of so much of our sexual behavior, that genes will ultimately determine the way sexual orientation is expressed (i.e., in the phenotype)?

A GENETIC SCENARIO

I believe the answer is yes and no.

Let's assume the simplest genetic scenario, where sexual orientation is a one-gene trait with a straight allele and a gay allele [Alleles are simply different versions of a given gene, like two different brands of spark plugs in a car, or two different makes of a silicon chip—they do basically the same job, but may perform slightly differently], and heterosexuality is dominant over homosexuality, which is to say, the straight allele is stronger, or has more votes, than the gay allele. I suspect that, for those men who are "homozygous recessive"—both copies of their sexual orientation are gay—their genotypes predispose them to a sexual responsivity that is same-sex oriented, what [researcher] Alfred Kinsey would have labelled "primarily or exclusively homosexual." These are men who typically have engaged in gender nonconforming play as children or who have known from an early age that they were "different" from other little boys in some significant way. Despite the influences of a strongly heterosexual environment and of interacting biological and cognitive processes, these individuals remain true to their genetic endowment and experience their sexual orientation as undeniably gay. Regardless of whether or not these men choose to express this trait or to engage in same-sex behavior, their sexual "connection" to others will always be a same-sex one.

By contrast, there are those men who are homozygous dominant—both of their alleles are straight—and will thus only experience a sexual attraction to women. Although they could conceivably experiment with same-sex behaviors, they would never feel the same sexual or romantic connection experienced by those with a same-sex genetic predisposition, despite their experimentation.

Considering just these two groups of males, we arrive at what several geneticists argue to be a rather compelling, largely bimodal distribution of this trait among all men, i.e., a J-curve with a preponderance of males self-identifying as nongay, a minority self-identifying as gay, and an even smaller percentage self-identifying as bisexual. I would like to suggest, however, that the apparently bimodal distribution of this trait may in fact be an artifact of self-reporting by a number of men who, despite some degree of same-sex attraction, dishonestly identify themselves as nongay. Certainly the adverse climate in our culture toward gay men would explain why there would be such a reluctance toward more honest self-reporting. But who are these men, and what about those few who identify as bisexual?

INCOMPLETE DOMINANCE OF TRAITS

Currently popular genetic explanations of sexual orientation fall short in answering this question, as well as such questions as (a) among monozygous [identical] twins, why isn't there a 100% concordance rate of homosexuality, and (b) how do you account for those straight siblings of gay brothers and sisters, since they share the same genetic map (genotype)? Perhaps these questions might best be answered by abandoning genetic models of sexual orientation that suggest that a gay gene's recessive nature can only be expressed phenotypically if the genotype is homozygous recessive. Under such models, individuals with a heterozygous genotype would therefore be heterosexually oriented. However, if we consider a model where sexual orientation results from a genetics of incomplete dominance, greater explanatory power results.

MULTIPLE FACTORS AFFECT SEXUAL ORIENTATION

The clearest evidence for multiple factors come from the genetic studies. These offer very strong evidence that genes play a role in influencing sexual orientation, at least in men, but equally they demonstrate that genes are not the whole story. It may be that the genetic influence is very strong or even total in some families, and weak or absent in others. Alternatively, it may be that all gay men have some genetic predisposition toward homosexuality, and this has combined with other predisposing factors to lead to an actual homosexual outcome.

Simon LeVay, *Queer Science*, 1996.

Consider the trait for human hair type. The dominant allele is for curly hair, whereas the recessive allele is for straight hair. However a heterozygous allele pair (one for curly, one for straight) produces wavy hair, an intermediate phenotype. Within this model, one could argue that men who were homozygous dominant for sexual orientation would experience heterosexual attractions, those who were homozygous recessive would experience homosexual attractions, and those who were heterozygous for sexual orientation would experience an incomplete genetic predisposition in their sexual orientation. Consequently, this third group of men would prove more susceptible in their sexual development than the other two groups to the many biological (e.g., prenatal hormonal influences, temperaments), environmental (e.g., parenting, childhood play), and cognitive (e.g., attitude formation, curiosity) factors that have been linked with sexual orientation.

It is this group, therefore, who genotypically are predisposed as bisexual (i.e., heterozygous) but who phenotypically experience their sexual orientation as either heterosexual, homosexual, or bisexual, depending upon a host of non-genetic factors encountered during development. Given the strong heterosexual thrust of our culture, it is not surprising that most of these men develop a nongay sexual orientation. But, for some of these men, sexual orientation may prove a much more ambivalent experience, and, despite the way they privately experience their sexual orientation, many will be inclined to publicly report their sexual orientation as heterosexual, thus yielding the typically high gay/nongay distribution of the trait in research studies. However, I contend that it may very well be within this group that we find the so-called "glitches" and exceptions in research who have been viewed somewhat suspiciously, if not downright incredulously by gay and nongay individuals alike—bisexuals, "late bloomers," and homoerotic-fantasizing heterosexuals (see, for example, Henry Adams et al.'s 1996 article in the *Journal of Abnormal Psychology*, in which a group of highly homophobic, exclusively heterosexual men became sexually aroused when exposed to gay male erotica), to mention a few.

Given this genetic model which allows for incomplete dominance of the trait, we seem to have greater flexibility in explaining examples of sexual orientation that have changed over time, or which defy the "you're either gay or you're straight" categorization. It is easier because an incomplete dominance of the trait suggests a stronger influence of environment, biology, and cognition than one might suspect for those possessing stronger and more clearly defined genetic influences (i.e., homozygous carriers).

Yes, I do agree that sexual orientation is most definitely the result of genetics in gay and straight men, but I'm arguing that its role may prove less influential for a third group, bisexuals. In any event, be we geneticists, psychologists, or social constructionists, I urge that we resist too narrowly restricting our range of vision as we study this rather perplexing phenomenon called sexual orientation.

| "We don't need to find the cause of
homosexuality. Being gay or lesbian
is not something that has to be
justified."

THE CAUSES OF HOMOSEXUALITY
ARE IRRELEVANT

Erin Blades

In the following viewpoint, Erin Blades argues that the search
for a "gay gene" is rooted in homophobia—a fear of homosexuality. If homosexuality were not generally considered abnormal
and immoral, she points out, the search for its causes would not
be so intense. Furthermore, she contends, the discovery of a gay
gene would not necessarily lead society to accept homosexuality
as natural and normal; people might simply conclude that homosexuality is a genetic defect. Ultimately, Blades maintains, the
basis of sexual orientation is unimportant. Gays and lesbians deserve societal acceptance rooted in a respect for individual differences—a kind of support that does not require knowledge
about homosexuality's causes, she concludes. Blades is a freelance writer.

As you read, consider the following questions:

1. What were the results of Simon LeVay's brain research,
   according to Blades?
2. In the author's opinion, why has there been no search for a
   genetic cause for left-handedness?
3. What is the key to ending homophobia, in Blades's opinion?

Reprinted from Erin Blades, "The Gay Gene: What Does It Matter?" *The Peak*, February
1996, by permission of *The Peak*.

Homosexuality has been viewed as "abnormal" for centuries. Although it is more accepted today than ever, it is still not "normal" to many people. Religious moralists think homosexuality is a sin, the willful choice of evil. Strict behaviourists think it is a mental disorder resulting from ineffective parenting. Others just think it's wrong.

Simon LeVay, a neuroanatomist at the Salk Institute in La Jolla, California, examined the brains of 41 people—including 19 homosexual men who had died of AIDS-related illnesses—and discovered a genetic difference between gay and straight men. Since his research was made public, most people have come to believe that homosexuality is genetic.

LeVay discovered that the area of the brain believed to be responsible for sexual activity was less than half the size in gay men than in heterosexual men. (One question, does that mean that a lesbian's brain is the same size as a straight guy's?) This was the first direct evidence of a correlation between sexual orientation and brain structure. Although I think homosexuality is genetic, it doesn't matter to me. It's not going to change my opinion of myself. I'm okay with who I am. The only way the discovery of a gay gene would be important to me is if it puts an end to homophobia.

A HOMOPHOBIC SEARCH

The search for the gay gene is itself homophobic. Instead of just accepting the fact that some people are straight and some people are lesbian, gay, or bisexual, people are searching for a cause—as if homosexuality is a disease. Nobody's looking for the heterosexual gene. Nobody's trying to find a genetic cause for left-handedness, which could even be less prevalent than homosexuality and therefore even more "abnormal." My mom is left-handed. Maybe her parents did something wrong. Maybe she's got a disease. But people don't really think of being left-handed in that way. It's not a big deal because left-handedness, like heterosexuality, is considered natural. . . . Homosexuality isn't considered natural. That's why a cause is being searched for.

Confirmation of a genetic cause for homosexuality won't change people's attitudes toward gay people. It won't make homophobia go away. The fact that we can't help being gay is supposed to make people go, "Well, if they can't help it then it's okay." Why do we have to prove that our same-sex attraction is not something we can control? The implication is that if homosexuality were controllable, it would or should be controlled. If that's not homophobia, I don't know what is.

Still, I can see how it might be tempting for people—straight or gay—to embrace the idea. If a gay gene is discovered, then we can claim it's like being left-handed. We'd be acting as nature intended and could then expect equal treatment. The gay gene might mean an end to all of the standard arguments used to block our legal rights and may be enough to persuade legislators that discrimination on the basis of sexual orientation is unconstitutional. Parents might not be afraid if their kids have a gay teacher, and adoption agencies might be less reluctant to let gay couples adopt kids. They wouldn't be worried that the kids are going to grow up gay because homosexuality is not contagious.

But would that really fix anything? People might be forced to tolerate us, but it wouldn't make them accept us. What makes us think that given how cruel and punitive so many have been towards us that the gay gene won't be seen as pathological? To a lot of people we'd still be mutants, just not social mutants any more. We'd be genetic mutants. We'd be able to claim that homosexuality is no different than skin colour or left-handedness, but our opponents could claim that instead of a natural gene, it is a genetic defect. That doesn't do much for gay and lesbian liberation, does it?

The question of cause should be irrelevant. If more people believed that homosexuality is as natural and normal as heterosexuality, no one would want or need to search for a cause.

The Root of Homophobia

The root of homophobia is sex. Sex. Sex. Sex. A huge issue for a lot of people. Most of the big social debates have to do with sex. Prostitution, pornography, lap dancing, nudity. Most people agree with the current regulation of such aspects of our sexuality, but others disagree. Sex is controversial territory. It fascinates us. I'm sure the first thing people think of when I say I'm gay is "Hey. She sleeps with girls!"

When I say I'm gay, I'm not just talking about who I sleep with. It's not what I do, it's who I am. It's so much more than sex. Even outside the bedroom my identity as a lesbian colours every aspect of my life. If people weren't so concerned about sex (especially homosexual sex), we wouldn't be hunting for the gay gene.

The key to ending homophobia is making people understand and accept that sex is only one aspect of being gay or lesbian. When we talk about straight relationships, the conversation is not centered around sex. We talk about marriage, love, and how Men are from Mars, Women are from Venus. Heterosexuality is socially organized as natural and normal. Gays and lesbians are social outcasts.

The heterosexual hegemony that dominates our society marginalizes same-sex relationships. Because of this hegemony, we've been fired, beaten, spit at, called names, threatened and made to feel ashamed of who we are. We've all been oppressed in one way or another and often without legal protection or recourse.

"THIS PROVES IT... THERE IS ALSO A GENETIC LINK TO HOMOPHOBIA..."

Bill Schorr. Reprinted by permission of United Feature Syndicate, Inc.

Our relationships are different from but equivalent to their heterosexual counterparts. Love is just as important. So is marriage. People need to realize this. Therefore, it is important for us to come out and defend our identity. It is important that we challenge the heterosexual hegemony. But we need to go beyond simply proclaiming our identity and creating our own community. We need to directly challenge sexual regulation in our society and shatter the rigid sex and gender rules that bind us all.

NORMALIZING SAME-SEX RELATIONSHIPS

Mainstream media usually reproduce the heterosexual norm by excluding gay and lesbian characters and issues. However, considerable media attention has been devoted to gay and lesbian themes in the last few years. Two American primetime television shows, *Roseanne* and *Friends*, feature homosexual characters. A group of Canadian artists known collectively as "Kiss and Tell" have produced two very important books (*Drawing the Line* and *Her*

Tongue on My Theory) that explore lesbian sexuality truthfully and without reservation. Canadian documentary filmmaker David Adkin has produced a film called *Jim Loves Jack: The James Egan Story* which celebrates the 45-year marriage and landmark constitutional rights struggle of Jim Egan and Jack Nesbit.

It is not only important for us to see ourselves represented accurately by mainstream media. It is also important for heterosexuals to see accurate portrayals as well. This sort of positive media attention normalizes gay and lesbian relationships because they are dealt with honestly, openly and without prejudice. Such treatment includes and affirms our identities and paves the way for acceptance, not just tolerance. Media efforts like this are important because they normalize same-sex relationships, and if people see homosexuality as normal, they won't need to search for a gay gene, or any other cause for homosexuality.

Justification Is Not Necessary

Still, scientists continue to hunt for a cause for homosexuality, as if being gay is something bad or defective. People are all too willing to accept this. Maybe it's because it reaffirms their own heterosexual lifestyles. If gay is bad then heterosexuality is good. If heterosexuality is the norm then anything different is "abnormal." If something is abnormal then there must be a reason.

It doesn't surprise me that when I first talked to my mom and dad about being gay, the first question they asked was "why?" After listening in shocked silence for nearly an hour, my dad cleared his throat and asked "Why do you think you're gay? What do you think caused it?"

I had just spent an hour basically telling them how happy I was, and they wanted to know why—as if I couldn't possibly be happy this way. As if there were something wrong with me. I stared at them in disbelief. "What?" I asked, "nothing caused it!" and continued to talk happily about my life, hoping they'd realize it doesn't matter.

Gays and lesbians are still fighting the heterosexual hegemony, both within our own families and in society at large. The fact that people think it's necessary to find the cause of homosexuality is evidence of this fight. We don't need to find the cause of homosexuality. Being gay or lesbian is not something that has to be justified. We need to get more support based simply on open-minded acceptance of individual differences, regardless of whether it is a difference by choice or by physiology. The end to homophobia will not come through science.

7

| "Science has a significant role to play in helping create a more gay-friendly world."

THE CAUSES OF HOMOSEXUALITY ARE NOT IRRELEVANT

Simon LeVay

Simon LeVay, a neurobiologist, is cofounder of the Institute of Gay and Lesbian Education in West Hollywood, California. He is the author of several books, including *The Sexual Brain* and *Queer Science*. In 1991, LeVay claimed to have found a link between brain structure and homosexuality. He argues in the following viewpoint that sexual-orientation research is important because scientific evidence could convince more people that homosexuality is an inborn quality. Ultimately, knowledge about the causes of homosexuality could actually increase societal acceptance of gays and lesbians, LeVay concludes.

As you read, consider the following questions:

1. What was the author's reason for pursuing research into the causes of homosexuality?
2. What are the implications of a blood test that indicates homosexuality, in LeVay's opinion?
3. According to LeVay, why did an antigay newspaperman in Arizona change his mind about homosexuality?

At Levitican University, a fundamentalist Christian college in Southern California, something remarkable is going on. Professor Guy Albrick, head of the Department of Molecular Neurology, has devised a radically new technique to help male students who are troubled by homosexual urges. In a pioneering experiment he grafted genetically engineered nerve cells into the hypothalamus of their brains, which assemble themselves into circuitry that generates opposite-sex attraction.

Over a period of weeks following the operation he discovered an extraordinary behavioural change in his human guinea pigs. The men gradually began to lose their desire for other men; some even began spontaneously dating women, their homosexuality apparently a thing of the past.

Recently, Albrick has gone one better. He has put his nerve cells into a "vaccine" that he routinely (and secretly) inoculates into the cadets in Levitican's officer-training corps. It's an anti-gay prophylaxis: the idea is to eliminate any tendency toward homosexual behaviour, which is strictly forbidden in the United States military.

Unfortunately, the vaccine seems to have been working too efficiently: a number of the injected cadets, now members of the armed forces, have been arrested for rape, gay-bashing, and other crimes of violence. A tide of heterosexual male aggression has been unleashed which nobody seems able to control. . .

This is fiction, of course, the plot of my techno-thriller *Albrick's Gold*. But could it become fact? And if so, what should we be doing about it? If it ever does become fact, I'll have to take part of the blame. For it was my research, published in 1991, which suggested that brain structure—particularly the size of a tiny cell group in the hypothalamus, where our sexual urges may have their roots—helps to determine whether a person is straight, gay, or bisexual. At that time, I was a neurobiologist at the Salk Institute in San Diego and deeply immersed in questions of brain organisation and development. And I was gay. So it wasn't a big stretch to put these two parts of my life together: to ask whether this particular aspect of human diversity, so central to my own sense of identity and my place in society, could be understood in terms of neurons, synapses, and genes.

CAUGHT IN THE CROSSFIRE

My interest, I think, was an innocent one—I was just plain curious about it. I had no agenda, and no concern about what my work might lead to, other than to a better understanding of what makes us human. I didn't even think my research would attract much public attention. I was, in fact, your typical ivory-tower scientist.

But when my research hit the headlines, everyone assumed I did have an agenda, although they couldn't agree on what it was. To some, I was out to pathologise, perhaps to eliminate, homosexuality. "Another example of medical homophobia!" declared one gay academic on prime-time television. To others, I was out to justify homosexuality—to prove that we're "born that way" and therefore not to blame for our sexual urges or our sexual behaviour. I felt like I was caught in the crossfire.

Over the years since I published my research I've had time to look back on it and reflect on its implications. From having been a scientist immersed in his work I have now become more of an observer concerned about its consequences.

What I've come up with is the following: first, I believe I was right to study this question for its own sake. That's how the best science is done—the ivory tower is there for a purpose, after all. And if, as I've always believed, there's nothing inferior, bad, or sick about being either gay or straight, then there can be nothing wrong with studying how people become one or the other.

"Curing" Homosexuality?

In many people's minds, though, homosexuality and gay people are inferior. And these people might want to use scientific findings to "cure" us, to weed us out, or even to prevent us from being born. Lord Jacobovitz, for example, then Chief Rabbi of the United Kingdom, reacted to news of my research by saying: "If we could by some form of genetic engineering eliminate these trends, we should—so long as it is done for a therapeutic purpose." (His ethics adviser later made it clear that the therapeutic programme was to be a voluntary one.) How likely is it that such a technology will become a reality? A few years ago, I would have said that it could never happen, but now I'm not so sure.

Recently, researchers have succeeded in changing the behaviour of laboratory animals by grafting nerve cells into their hypothalamus. This wasn't in the sphere of sex, but in that of circadian rhythms: animals that were bred to have an abnormally short, 20-hour sleep/wake cycle were switched to a 24-hour cycle by grafting brain cells from "normal" animals into them. It may not be such a great leap from that to changing the direction of a person's sexual desire.

What's really made these prospects seem more immediate and threatening is the molecular genetic research into sexuality:

specifically, the research of Dean Hamer and his colleagues at the National Cancer Institute in Washington.

In 1993 Hamer's group reported evidence that genes on the X chromosome predispose boys to become either gay or straight. The genes haven't been identified yet, but if Hamer's findings are right, it won't be more than a few years before they are. And then it will be a simple matter to develop a blood test that could be applied to adults, to children, even to foetuses.

The test won't be wholly accurate, of course, since genes are by no means the entire reason why an individual is gay or straight (even identical twins can have different orientations). But they'll be accurate enough, in many people's minds, to justify pre-employment testing, pre-marital testing, and pre-insurance testing. Accurate enough to counsel a child—to help stiffen his resistance to his gay tendencies, perhaps. And certainly accurate enough to abort a foetus, at least in countries like the US, where it's permissible to abort for any reason or none.

PREVENTING GENETIC ABUSES

Dean Hamer is concerned enough about these dangers that he wants to restrict the use of genetic tests for homosexuality. "We believe that it would be fundamentally unethical," he has written, "to use such information to try to assess or alter a person's current or future sexual orientation."

Hamer takes these fears of the misuse of "gay genes" sufficiently seriously to have proposed a drastic solution. He talks of patenting the relevant DNA sequences, thus preventing the commercial development of blood tests. At best, however, this could only put off the crisis for the lifetime of a patent.

I take a more libertarian view. I am equally concerned about possible abuses, but I don't think that legal restrictions are either a practical or an ethical way to prevent them. I believe that we can only prevent such abuses by creating a society in which gays and lesbians are valued—valued as individuals and valued as a group of people who make a unique contribution to society.

But beyond the possible abuses, there's another aspect to "queer science" that could have unexpected beneficial effects. For the biological findings reinforce what most gays and lesbians feel about themselves—that their sexual orientation is something given, an attribute that helps define their core identity, not a mere set of behaviours that a person chooses to engage in or not as whim or morality may dictate.

To many readers, this may not seem like a surprising assertion. But to about half the population of the US, according to national polls, homosexuality is seen as "something one chooses to be". And it is with this half of the population that the strongest anti-gay sentiment is lodged.

This debate about the nature of homosexuality and research into its biological roots has been most urgent in the US where Christian fundamentalists and gay rights activists have long been at each other's throats. Under US law, the extent to which any minority group is entitled to the state's protection depends in part on whether the group is defined by some innate characteristic or whether it is a voluntary association. Thus, black Americans have more legal protection against discrimination than the Boy Scouts.

HOMOSEXUALITY WILL PERSIST

Barring almost unimaginable shifts in human psychology, sexual science, and society, there is no reason to believe that there will cease to be men and women with homoerotic interests. There will continue to be, that is, some analogue of gay identity in the future, regardless of whether that identity is socially closeted in nature, fully incorporated into society at every level, or something else. Even the most aggressive "search and destroy" program using prenatal diagnostics and interventions would reach only a portion of the world's population and would not obstruct all the mechanisms by which people come to have homoerotic interests and behaviors. Sexual orientation therapies would remain unwanted by the vast majority of gay and lesbian adults. Questions of the just social treatment of gay people must remain, therefore, very much on the moral agenda. We are long since past the time in which medical professionals or moralists can reflexively invoke the vision of a future with no gay people in it.

Timothy F. Murphy, *Gay Science*, 1997.

It follows that gays and lesbians would be entitled to relatively little support if being gay is something optional. But what if gayness is inborn? Dean Hamer tried to sum it up: "Since people don't choose their genes, they couldn't possibly choose their sexual orientation."

HOW SCIENCE COULD HELP

There has been a trend in the US to treat gays and lesbians as a discrete class of citizens, rather like an ethnic group, entitled to protection from discrimination on the basis of their sexual orientation.

In 1996, for example, the US Senate came within a single vote of granting gays and lesbians federal protection from discrimination in employment. Again, the debate on the Senate floor reflected divergent beliefs about gay people. Senator Ted Kennedy, the bill's sponsor, spoke of us as a disadvantaged minority; his opponents referred to us as "people who choose to engage in that lifestyle".

Over and over, during the past few years, I have seen how intimately beliefs about the nature and cause of homosexuality affect attitudes toward gays and lesbians. I hear the same thing over and over: if being gay is a choice, we're free to make our own judgments about gay people; if it's not, then whatever we think about the rights and wrongs of same-sex behaviour, gays and lesbians are entitled to some respect, some understanding, some space.

Often, I want to say: forget about science, forget about reasons, just treat us as human beings, as your neighbours, as your children. In the end, hopefully, that's how it will be. But in the meantime, people need reasons. One man, an Arizona newspaperman who had been writing anti-gay editorials for many years, changed his mind after reading some scientific articles about homosexuality.

"I became persuaded it was not something voluntary," he said, "not something you embraced, it was the way you were born. If it's the way you were born then it ceases to be a sin, and then one's whole theological and moral perspective shifts, and then you begin to view the problem entirely differently, and that's what happened to me." He retracted his earlier views and urged the city of Phoenix to pass a gay-rights ordinance, something that actually came to pass soon afterward.

Examples like this suggest that science has a significant role to play in helping create a more gay-friendly world. But we're not there yet. In the meantime, watch out for zombie-like Leviticans with holes in their heads.

PERIODICAL BIBLIOGRAPHY

The following articles have been selected to supplement the diverse views presented in this chapter. Addresses are provided for periodicals not indexed in the *Readers' Guide to Periodical Literature*, the *Alternative Press Index*, the *Social Sciences Index*, or the *Index to Legal Periodicals and Books*.

Tina Adler	"Animals' Fancies," *Science News*, January 4, 1997.
Chandler Burr	"Why Conservatives Should Embrace the Gay Gene," *Weekly Standard*, December 16, 1996. Available from News America Publishing, Inc., 1211 Avenue of the Americas, New York, NY 10036.
William Byne	"Varieties of Biological Explanation," *Harvard Gay & Lesbian Review*, Winter 1997.
John Gallagher	"Gay for the Thrill of It," *Advocate*, February 17, 1998.
Ted Gideonse	"The Sexual Blur," *Advocate*, June 24, 1997.
Carla Golden	"Do Women Choose Their Sexual Identity?" *Harvard Gay & Lesbian Review*, Winter 1997.
Al Gore	"The Genetic Moral Code," *Advocate*, March 31, 1998.
Denise Grady	"The Brains of Gay Men," *Discover*, January 1992.
John Leland and Mark Miller	"Can Gays 'Convert'?" *Newsweek*, August 17, 1998.
Simon LeVay	"A Difference in Hypothalamic Structure Between Heterosexual and Homosexual Men," *Science*, August 30, 1991.
Mordecai Richler	"Unnatural Selection," *Saturday Night*, May 1997.
Byron York	"Hyping the Gay Gene," *Forbes Media Critic*, Spring 1996. Available from Forbes Inc., 60 Fifth Ave., New York, NY 10011.

Do Homosexuals
Face Serious
Discrimination?

CHAPTER PREFACE

The proposed Employment Non-Discrimination Act (ENDA), a bill first introduced into Congress in 1994, would include sexual orientation among the federal laws that prohibit workplace discrimination on the basis of race, religion, gender, national origin, age, and disability. Controversy surrounding ENDA, which had not passed as of December 1998, typically focuses on whether such legislation would grant gays and lesbians equal rights and opportunities or give them special rights and unfair privileges.

Supporters of ENDA maintain that gay people face pervasive discrimination in the workplace. When compared with heterosexuals of the same age and educational background, gay men earn between 11 and 27 percent less and lesbians make as much as 30 percent less, contends Cornell University instructor Anna Marie Smith. Moreover, ENDA proponents report, a *Wall Street Journal* poll found that 66 percent of Fortune 500 executives "would hesitate to give a management job to a homosexual." To avoid discrimination, many gay people feel forced to "closet" themselves—hide their sexual identity—on the job, ENDA supporters contend. Such behavior, many argue, is psychologically burdensome for gays and lesbians and damages the workplace by building walls between coworkers. Passing ENDA would help to mitigate these effects of homophobia and promote equal rights for gay people, supporters maintain.

Critics argue that a new antidiscrimination law is unnecessary because homosexuals already enjoy the same civil rights protections that heterosexuals do. Same-sex attraction, they contend, is not an obvious characteristic, such as skin color, that distinguishes homosexuals as a group. As columnist Mona Charen puts it, "Forbidding discrimination against gays is like forbidding discrimination against mystery readers—how does an employer know?" Moreover, ENDA opponents maintain, the claim that homosexuals face economic discrimination is false. According to journalist Justin Raimondo, gay male couples earn an average annual income of $51,325—significantly higher than the average household income of $36,520. The main objection to ENDA, however, is that it could require employers who morally object to homosexuality to intentionally hire gay people. Such a scenario would grant special privileges to gays while infringing on the rights of those who support traditional values, critics contend.

Claims of antigay discrimination are the subject of intense debate. The viewpoints in the following chapter further explore these issues.

| "Homosexuals constitute a legitimate
minority in respect to their
demographics and life experiences in
an oppressive society."

HOMOSEXUALS ARE AN OPPRESSED MINORITY

Brian R. Allen

Homosexuals face oppression that is comparable to the discrimination experienced by women and ethnic minorities, argues Brian R. Allen in the following viewpoint. Like other minorities, gays and lesbians encounter discrimination in housing and in employment, the author points out. Moreover, Allen contends, homosexuality has been stigmatized as abnormal or subhuman, making gays and lesbians targets for societal disapproval and violence. Presently, gays and lesbians still struggle to attain respect, healthy identities, and equal rights, the author maintains. Allen is a freelance writer.

As you read, consider the following questions:

1. For what reasons does the military discharge known homosexuals, according to Allen?
2. According to the author, what are the results of society's failure to legitimize gay relationships?
3. In Allen's opinion, how have right-wing groups used gay pride parades to promote their own agendas?

Abridged from Brian R. Allen, "Do Homosexuals Constitute a Legitimate Minority?" web article at www.sonoma.edu/Depts/AMCS/upstream/gay.html, 1996. Reprinted by permission of the author.

G ays and lesbians have been a part of human experience since time began, crossing every racial, ethnic, religious, cultural, and social group. To what extent do homosexuals constitute a legitimate minority group in American society? Many factions in our society believe homosexuality to be "just a phase" or even more insidious, a "mental disorder" likened to drug addiction. I will prove that homosexuals are indeed a minority group. I will accomplish this by comparing and contrasting the homosexual/lesbian experience with that of other oppressed peoples in American society and demonstrate parallels. I fully realize that no two minority groups completely and exactly parallel each other in the degrees of oppression; however, the thesis of this viewpoint is that homosexuals constitute a legitimate minority in respect to their demographics and life experiences in an oppressive society. . . .

The definition of a minority, according to Webster's Dictionary, is "a racial, religious, ethnic or political group that differs from the larger, controlling group." That controlling group is white, heterosexual, and male. This group forms the infrastructure: a patriarchal society in the United States that all minorities must maneuver through in their daily lives.

THE GAY POPULATION

Estimates of the population of the homosexual community range wildly from 10 million to 40 million (5%–20%), "an elusive figure simply because the overwhelming majority of homosexuals do not, and for good reason, affirm this fact in public." Most gays and lesbians agree with the famous Kinsey report of the 1950s which put the population at 10% (slightly under the African-American population of 12%). Like African-Americans, Asians, and Native Americans, homosexual numbers are politically significant in legislative policies affecting minorities. Many conservative right-wing factions downplay homosexual numbers to around 1% to minimize their role in society and their needs in the minds of the voting public. Why should a voter waste precious energy and tax money on a minority that represents only 1% of the population? Gays and lesbians differ from other minorities because they are not discernible by their phenotypes, or physical characteristics. Homosexuals cross every racial and ethnic group. They are brought together by oppression and common life experiences. Many ethnic gay men experience double discrimination; and ethnic lesbians face triple discrimination by being of a different ethnicity, gay, and women.

The gay community parallels African-Americans' experience

with discrimination in certain areas. In the 1940s, blacks were segregated from whites in the U.S. armed forces because, according to the military, their integration would have distracted and interfered with the morale of the white troops. Flash to the election year of 1992, when candidate Bill Clinton vows to the gay community to lift the ban on homosexuals in the military if elected. President Clinton does indeed attempt to lift the ban, but eventually gives in to right-wing and Pentagon opposition by adopting the half-hearted policy of Don't-Ask-Don't-Tell. This policy utilizes society's most powerful form of segregation for homosexuals: the closet. Thousands of worthy homosexual soldiers are discharged every year due to the military's ban. The military's reasoning parallels that of 50 years ago: loss of morale and instability in the ranks. The fact remains that homosexuals are already in the military. The military just needs to acknowledge their presence without segregating them with unjust discharges. In addition, homosexuals, like African-Americans, face discrimination in housing. Many landlords refuse to rent to gays and lesbians, whether they're "out of the closet" or not. Suspicion of being gay can cause a refusal of residence as well. Consequently, homosexuals, like other minorities in large cities, will tend to cluster to form enclaves or ghettos. The Castro District and the Fillmore District in San Francisco are examples of clustering for homosexuals and African-Americans, respectively. Gays and lesbians are thus exploited in these clusters, ". . . landlords charge more than the houses and apartments would ordinarily be worth and make large profits from gay people who want or need to live among supportive neighbors." What has occurred is a very segregated society, drawn along minority and ethnic lines.

INSTITUTIONALIZED DISCRIMINATION

Institutionalized racism and sexism occurs when social and political structures within society reinforce and support the actions of a perceived superior group. This discrimination has become so culturally ingrained and pervasive, its perpetrators often don't realize discrimination has occurred. The end result denies ethnic minorities and women employment and advancement economically. For example, "whites are almost seven times as likely to hold a job at the top of the economy than blacks." However, only homosexuals are specifically barred from many jobs (social work, clergy, teaching, the armed forces, and many government jobs) ". . . from fear that hiring someone openly gay would drive away business or that we will physically molest people left to our attention—children or patients." The myth of gay molesters persists despite several studies which have shown that the majority of molestations are committed by heterosexual men, usually involving a family member. The Boy Scouts' denial of gay, male troop leaders is a clear example of this pervasive and insidious myth. What has occurred resembles a caste system in America, developed by and for white, heterosexual males, where ethnic minorities and gays are barred from certain occupations.

Discrimination occurs in [various] ways. For instance, homosexual relationships aren't legitimized like heterosexual relationships. Homosexuals can be barred from seeing a sick or dying partner. They have no claim to their partner's property after death, no custody rights of the deceased partner's children, and receive no tax breaks for being married (although now some companies and states do offer domestic partners benefits). Furthermore, lesbian mothers can have their children taken away from them, gay aliens must deny their homosexuality upon entering the country, and many gay and lesbian legislators choose to remain in the closet for fear of their constituents suspecting they are gay. "The net result is to encourage the closeted to stay that way for fear of not being protected."

CIVIL DISOBEDIENCE

The 1960s revealed another parallel between homosexuals and minorities. The Gay Liberation Movement began along with the rise of the Black Civil Rights Movement, the American Indian Movement, and the Feminist Movement. "Blacks had created a mood for justice and a mood of militancy . . . [and] expanded the tactics of dissent and made protest legitimate." The gay activist movement began after the infamous Stonewall riots, when gay men refused to submit to a routine New York City police raid at the Greenwich Village bar.

Like other minorities, equal rights were not handed to homosexuals on a silver platter. They had to be fought for. The Constitution does not declare that homosexuality is a crime. However, at one time statutes in every state have made oral and anal intercourse illegal (for both heterosexuals and homosexuals). The majority of people arrested for these crimes have been homosexual men. This makes homosexuals ". . . unapprehended criminals in every state." Due to the Gay and Women's Liberation Movements, along with research on human sexuality, consciousness has been raised. By 1975, eight states had decriminalized the illegal sex acts. Several cities passed anti-discrimination ordinances specifically for gay people.

In addition, Rep. Bella Abzug (D-NY) in 1975 introduced legislation to amend the 1964 Civil Rights Act by adding ". . . affectional or sexual preference to race, religion and sex as areas of proscription against discrimination." Abzug was backed by many professional organizations, including the American Civil Liberties Union (ACLU). The Act has yet to be amended, but continues to be introduced every year.

With the advent of AIDS in the early 1980s, a resurgence of gay activism arose to fight the complacency of the Reagan administration. Radical activist groups, such as AIDS Coalition to Unleash Power (ACT-UP) and Queer Nation, evolved to gain national and governmental attention by charging that "...promising AIDS drugs weren't being tested, drug trials excluded women of color, and no individual in the government or medical establishment was taking the lead."

HOMOSEXUAL IDENTITY

As with other oppressed groups, homosexuals' identities are proscribed by the larger, controlling (heterosexual) majority. A need arose to explain homosexual behavior. Several reasons for this "deviant behavior" were developed: ". . . a defective or deficient parent or parents and resulting arrested development," strong mothers and weak fathers, fear of the opposite sex, or "just a phase." Homosexuality was even listed in the medical journals as a mental disorder (but has since been removed). All of these myths were used as causes of homosexuality.

Similarly, upon first contact, Africans differed from Europeans in so many ways that a need arose to explain their color. It was thought to be a defect or abnormal. Theories arose for this defect, such as: too much Equatorial sun, fornication with apes, and even leprosy. . . .

As an oppressed minority, people of color are treated much the same as gays. Their existence is denied, their history is ignored, and their identity is the butt of many jokes. The cumulative effect of these proscribed identities is that it makes both groups subhuman; therefore they are easier to ignore. Both gays and ethnic minorities are hired last and fired first and become easy targets for violence.

Furthermore, homosexuals' self identity is confused by trying to achieve the unattainable goal of a "normal" family. Since the heterosexual family is the dominant social organization, there is tremendous pressure on homosexuals to conform. This creates stress, anxiety and alienation. "In taking on a gay identity and living within the gay world, a person takes on a stigmatized identity and lives within a world rendered secret by that stigmatization." The cultural environment of that stigma causes a cognitive switch in many gays to either remain in the closet, or to live in two worlds by adjusting mentally whenever the situation is comfortable or safe.

THE OPPRESSION OF HOMOSEXUALS

Millions of Americans who watched the *Oprah Winfrey Show* on November 13, 1986, witnessed testimonies by two victims of homophobia; one victim had been stabbed and the other beaten and raped. Viewers heard a *gay basher* describe how, as a teenager, he and his friends hunted gay men and beat them with baseball bats. A more recent *Oprah Winfrey Show* episode (1994) in which teenagers were interviewed revealed that little had changed over the past eight years.

On April 30, 1994, the *New York Times* reported an antigay murder of a 44-year-old musician from a small Pennsylvania town; a 17-year-old 11th grader had beaten him to death. Homophobic acts of harassment and aggression take place everywhere, in big cities, small towns, schools, college campuses, the workplace, and the military.

Homosexuals have been oppressed in the same manner as other minority groups. J. Boswell argued that throughout European history the treatment of homosexuals has paralleled the treatment of Jews. The same laws the Nazis applied to Jews were also used against homosexuals. The tremendous hostility and violence toward homosexuals led to their persecution and extermination.

Hilda F. Besner and Charlotte I. Spungin, *Gay and Lesbian Students: Understanding Their Needs*, 1995.

Given this oppression, minorities and gays emerged in the 1960s and 1970s ready to create their own self identities and cast aside those proscribed for them. Minorities took the identities that were perceived as negative and the source of oppression, and empowered themselves. For example, African-Americans developed slogans and a mentality affirming that "Black is Beautiful." The "Afro" hairstyle became a symbol of ethnicity and "blackness," and many sought their African roots as well. For women in the 1970s, the Helen Reddy song "I Am Woman" became the anthem for the Feminist Movement which stated that females are equal to males. The Gay Liberation Movement demanded equality and respect: gays burnt wooden closets to protest the figurative closets they were forced in; they adopted the pink triangle used by Nazi Germany to brand the thousands of gays killed during the Holocaust; and the word "queer" became a self appointed term used by radical, gay groups like Queer Nation. By coopting negative terms and identities, these groups took the punch out of these remarks and empowered themselves.

ANTI-GAY VIOLENCE

Violence is another common experience faced by minorities. Because minorities have been dehumanized by myths and stereotypes, it becomes much easier to target them with verbal assaults and physical abuse. "Gays are assaulted, confined to jail, forced into psychiatric treatment and even murdered—all for simply being gay." Along with millions of Jews, thousands of gays were also killed during the Holocaust and branded with pink triangles. "Queer-bashing" is a popular sport for some men. The patriarchal society condones such behavior by looking the other way or administering minimal jail time and fines. (California has implemented "hate crimes" legislation that brings tougher sentences for those specifically targeting minorities.)

The advent of AIDS brought increased violence directed towards gays. Increased media exposure and condemnation for the disease was ubiquitous. In addition, AIDS was perceived as another product of homosexuals' "deviant lifestyle."

Whenever a minority group organizes and demands change, the dominant group will attempt to reassert the status quo. The Ku Klux Klan, patriarchal forces against women, and the well organized, conservative right wing are a few examples. Many Christian conservatives utilize the following passage from the Bible as justification to condemn gays and lesbians: "Thou shalt not lie with mankind, as with womankind: it is an abomination." Many "good" Christians regard this passage as their justification to attack homosexuals both verbally and physically. For example, Rev. Fred Phelps of Kansas routinely and cruelly protests at funerals of AIDS victims with signs declaring, "GOD HATES FAGS!" The Vatican reinforces this stance by its refusal to reexamine the position of the Roman Catholic Church on homosexuality (despite the fact that many in the priesthood are gay). Thus, the myth of deviance and abnormality is perpetuated. Violence is born out of that myth.

GAY AND MINORITY CULTURE

Culture is created by humans interacting within social organizations, social functions, and social structures, within a certain environment. Culture is what culture does. Despite the fact that gays cross every conceivable social, racial, and ethnic group, a distinct culture has evolved that was born out of oppression, discrimination, and common life experiences. . . .

Many political and social groups like ACT-UP, The Shanti Project, and The Names Project sprouted during the AIDS crisis to assist the gay community. Gay enclaves or ghettos developed in every major city which allowed homosexuals to eat, work, and play in a safe environment. Gay authors such as Oscar Wilde, Armistead Maupin, the late Randy Shilts, and Rita Mae Brown write of the common cultural experiences of gays and lesbians. In addition, many fashion trends began in San Francisco's Castro District or in New York's Greenwich Village to be later marketed to "mainstream" America; similar to how "baggies" or "countries" worn by African-Americans and Hispanics influenced fashion for mainstream society desiring the "urban look." Madonna's hit song, "Vogue," drew heavily from a Harlem drag queen pageant. Other gay artists like the Pet Shop Boys, Melissa Ethridge, and K.D. Lang continue to influence the recording industry. One needs only to glance at the Rap section in music stores to see the influence that African-American artists have had on middle-American culture (the Pillsbury Doughboy rapping a jingle is evidence of Rap's diffusion). . . .

Homosexuals' cultural influence is described in numerous films such as *Victor/Victoria*, *Longtime Companion*, *Priscilla: Queen of the Desert*, and *Claire of the Moon*. Although gays and many ethnic minorities have been represented in the motion picture industry, it hasn't always been in a positive light. African-Americans were generally depicted as the villain, the servant, or mammy (*Song of the South*, *Gone With the Wind*), while gays and lesbians are still generally portrayed as demented, sissies, or suicidal (*Cruising*, *Boys in the Band*, *Basic Instinct*).

Cultural traits may be widespread throughout minority culture, but it is important to stress that homosexuals, African-Americans, women, Hispanics, Native Americans, and Asian-Americans are not homogeneous populations. Although a commonality does exist, all of the cultural experiences are not equally shared or experienced in the populations. For example, many have come to judge homosexuals by the outrageous, celebratory display of the Gay Pride Parades. These parades represent a small fraction of the gay community who choose to participate. Inevitably, right-wing groups have documented very specific portions of these events in order to incriminate the entire gay and lesbian population as licentious fools (proscribing identity). I believe that Mardi Gras is analogous to Gay Pride

Parades; and if it [were] considered to be the sum total of the heterosexual lifestyle, it would indeed cause controversy. It must be stressed that these are celebrations. Diversity of culture is what makes life interesting and it should be celebrated.

A LEGITIMATE MINORITY

In conclusion, homosexuals do indeed constitute a legitimate minority. Gays' and lesbians' sheer numbers must be considered in the political arena and, although disputed, represent a population in size similar to African-Americans. In addition, homosexuals share common experiences of oppression and discrimination due to negative, proscribed identities that most other ethnic minorities can attest to. . . . Gay self identity, like other minority identities, is eschewed due to those proscribed identities which are hallmarks of an oppressive society. Homosexuals participated in the great social movements of the 1960's and 1970's and continue to struggle to this day for equality in legislation.

"Homosexuals as a group have never been denied their full civil rights."

HOMOSEXUALS ARE NOT AN OPPRESSED MINORITY

Elizabeth Wright

According to Elizabeth Wright, the author of the following viewpoint, homosexuals are not an oppressed minority. As a group, homosexuals have always had access to their full civil and constitutional rights, she maintains. In fact, Wright points out, homosexuals are generally more well educated and earn higher incomes than most heterosexual Americans. The claim that homosexuals face societal discrimination is made by homosexual lobbying groups in an attempt to gain sympathy and political status as "victims" in need of civil rights protections, Wright contends. She argues that homosexuals try to legitimize their abnormal sexual behavior by comparing themselves to blacks and other minority groups that have experienced injustice. Wright is the editor of *Issues & Views*, a quarterly journal that focuses on issues affecting the black community.

As you read, consider the following questions:

1. In Wright's opinion, why do black political elites ally themselves with the homosexual constituency?
2. According to the author, why did the American Psychiatric Association remove homosexuality from its list of sexual disorders?
3. How do the tactics of homosexual activists resemble the tactics of civil rights activists, in Wright's opinion?

Excerpted from Elizabeth Wright, "In the Name of 'Civil Rights,'" *Issues and Views*, Spring 1996. Reprinted by permission of the author.

As we blacks examine the frenetic activity of the homosexual lobby in this country, just one question need be asked. How is the effort to reconstitute our families and decimated communities served by any involvement with this interest group?

Of what value is it to us to assist homosexual activists in achieving their agenda, much of which is already well on the way to becoming fixtures in the country's social fabric? This agenda includes, among many items, the implementation of homosexual curriculum at all school levels, homosexual adoption of children (including access to foster care programs), supervisory access to all youth groups (homosexuals are now engaged in a legal battle with the Boy Scouts of America over this issue), the lowering of the age of consent for sex between children and adults, inclusion of sex-change operations in all universal health plans, open homosexuality in the military, and redefining the nature of the family, where for the first time in documented history, legal recognition is granted to "marriage" of members of the same sex.

Do you see anything in that list that could possibly benefit the cause of American blacks or inspire the alienated among us to higher endeavor? Apparently, our wise leadership does. True to their political chicanery, without benefit of referendum or poll, black elites continue to ally our cause with those who care nothing about the long-term progress of blacks. . . .

The reason behind these alliances is the same. Lacking any real financial power, black elites are truly powerless people. Except, that is, in the political sphere. It is here that they have carved out a niche for themselves that sometimes seems formidable.

Such power can be maintained, however, only by diligently working to widen the network of supporters and financial contributors. To maintain and expand their little bases of power, black leaders must ally with any constituency available, even if it wears the horns of the Devil.

HITCHING TO THE CIVIL RIGHTS STAR

When homosexual activists appeared on the public scene, some black leaders could hardly wait to offer up the cause of the black masses to the newest "social struggle" in town. Jesse Jackson was among the first to grandstand in demanding "justice" for the "gays." In 1981, Washington, DC's Mayor Marion Barry eagerly obliged the homosexual lobby by leading the drive to remove laws against sodomy from the books.

In 1993, over the protests of members of local chapters, the national board of the National Association for the Advancement of Colored People (NAACP) passed a resolution in support of homosexual advocates, thereby giving official support to the homosexual agenda. Blacks who picketed that year's NAACP annual convention, to oppose this action, were denounced by then executive director Benjamin Chavis as "rightwing reactionaries." In 1996, San Francisco's Mayor Willie Brown delighted in affirming and endorsing the homosexual agenda, and happily performed "marriage" ceremonies of same sex couples.

Homosexuals are no dummies. From the first, they recognized the advantage of hitching their wagon to the "civil rights" star. By asserting that their goal is to achieve their rights as citizens, and invoking the rhetoric of the 1960s, they touched a nerve in American society. Yet homosexuals as a group have never been denied their full civil rights.

No labor unions were ever formed to keep homosexuals out of the workplace, as was done to black men. No laws were put on books to stymie economic development and prevent the expansion of businesses beyond segregated communities. No regulations were ever concocted to keep homosexuals from voting. No laws ever forbade homosexuals from riding in the front of the bus.

HOMOSEXUALS RARELY FACE DISCRIMINATION

In spite of the fact that individual homosexuals sometimes face reprehensible behavior from roughnecks and bullies, as a group they are far from "oppressed." On the contrary, as a group, white homosexuals have always enjoyed their full constitutional rights. This is demonstrated by the fact that they enjoy higher than average incomes than most Americans, and they are more likely to hold advanced college degrees and more prestigious occupations than any other group.

In actuality, homosexuals are rarely discriminated against in the job market or when seeking housing, in spite of their anecdotal stories to the contrary. In most places, they have reputations as reliable workers and good rent-paying tenants. But the concept of "discrimination," which associates them with blacks and other "downtrodden" unfortunates, is a powerful one, guaranteed to arouse public sympathy.

The activist homosexual strives for the advantages that come with being officially recognized as a bona fide "protected minority" in America's weird patchwork of ethnic favoritism. Even without this designation, through dogged perseverance, homosexuals have intruded their political agenda into the platforms of major religious denominations, into the policies of major corporations and government agencies and, as we know, into the curriculums of schools and colleges around the country.

NORMALIZING A DISORDER

The organized homosexual lobby knows how to be tough. Toughness, and the threat of physical violence, was all it took to get the American Psychiatric Association (APA) to remove homosexuality from its list of sexual disorders. Throughout its history, this Association had diagnosed homosexuality as the aberrance that it is. The homosexual impulse was defined in medical circles as "an uncompleted gender identity seeking after its own sex to replace what was not fully developed." Medical journals were full of articles on the treatment of homosexuality.

But in the early 1970s, the homosexual lobby began to disrupt APA annual meetings and other gatherings, with an aim to force the organization to change its diagnosis in its official *Diagnostic and Statistics Manual.* Bullied and intimidated by constant threats of physical violence, in 1973, the APA issued its now infamous statement that more or less "normalizes" homosexuality and removed it from its diagnostic list of deviations.

This is how a psychiatric diagnosis came to be changed on the books. Not through years of scientific research, but through a vote taken under fear of mayhem and possible riots. As one APA member put it, "This was an action demanded by the ideological temper of the times."

Only one-third of the APA's psychiatrists voted on the measure and, needless to say, many have not changed their minds about the nature of homosexual behavior. In 1992, a group of psychologists and psychoanalysts formed NARTH (National Association for Research and Treatment of Homosexuality), to continue research into the disorder, and to provide therapy for individuals seeking a way out of the "gay lifestyle."

HOMOSEXUAL PRESSURE TACTICS

Not content with their victory in 1973, homosexual activists now work to prevent the availability of reorientation therapy to other homosexuals, even though it is practiced only when voluntarily sought. Every year, at annual meetings of each of the three professional associations—American Psychiatric, American Psychological and American Psychoanalytic—homosexuals introduce resolutions to condemn those who practice "sexual-conversion" therapy. They are determined to make it a crime for any therapist to counsel a patient who seeks help in dealing with a habit that the patient considers contrary to his own value system.

So far, these resolutions have been defeated by each professional organization when introduced. But it is probably only a matter of time before the pressures brought by the homosexual lobby will prevail. In the NARTH Bulletin of September 1995, Dr. Mark Stern writes, "Given the restrictive practice standards this resolution offers up, mental health providers would be at risk for possible professional liability actions if they treated what the APA—by political fiat in 1973 and not through scientific evaluation—now considers a non-disorder."

The homosexual who wishes to be freed from his abnormal behavior faces the possibility of a confrontation with the homosexual lobby. Anthony Falzarano, a member of an organization of former homosexuals, denounces political "gays" who work to coerce their agendas on scientific research organizations, and says, "For the American Psychological Association to even consider denying homosexuals the right to choose to seek help for their disorientation is outrageous and is baseless in science."

Psychiatrist Jeffrey Satinover, author of Homosexuality and the Politics of Truth, writes, "The debate over homosexuality has been profoundly affected by the current culture of complaint. Many areas of political, social and scientific life today are being profoundly influenced by the various competing claims to victimhood. The normalization of homosexuality was a classic example where the American Psychiatric Association knuckled under to a victim group's pressure tactics.". . .

EXAGGERATED RHETORIC

Homosexuals recognized early the advantage of linking the terms "racist" and "homophobe," in order to bring moral condemnation down on their enemies. In fact, since "racist" still carries greater moral condemnation, homosexuals very often will first accuse an opponent of racial bias, before publicly zapping him as a "homophobe."

The tactics of homosexual activists and civil rights activists are quite similar. Both groups specialize in the art of exaggerated rhetoric, accusing opponents of being "haters" or "gay bashers." Taking their cues from blacks who use the word "racist" to describe anyone who opposes their political demands, homosexuals push the envelope of overstatement.

To keep the indignation level high, a great many blacks are masters at stretching the borders of truth. According to them, putting an end to racially gerrymandered voting districts is the same as repealing the Voting Rights Act. And, challenging the racial bias of affirmative action programs is the same as desiring to revoke the citizenship of blacks, or, in their words, wanting to "roll back black progress" and "reinstitute slavery." In 1996, in Louisiana, when Governor Mike Foster, in a dispute over affirmative action, called the state's black leaders "shortsighted" for their adamant positions, he was condemned as a "racist" and "hater." In an attempt to defame his character, one black newspaper even dredged up negative data about Foster's grandfather who had served as the state's Governor in the 19th century!

Similarly, all those who challenge the homosexual lobby are deemed "gay bashers" and people filled with "hate." Violence against homosexuals is now any public opposition to their political agendas. So, when Pat Robertson on his 700 Club challenges aspects of "gay" demands, he demonstrates "hate against homosexuals."

When the head of a family rights group urges Americans to vote against certain referendums that would grant special status to homosexuals, he has committed a form of "violence against homosexuals." And when psychiatrists and other mental health providers treat homosexuals for their abnormality, they are practicing "genocide" against homosexuals.

The homosexual lobby strives to make criticism of homosexuality a "hate crime" in order to silence all opposition. Many of the laws that have been proposed, to stifle dissent, are vague and open to interpretation. If such laws are ever passed, homosexuals themselves would get to decide just what constitutes a "hate crime." Such laws are already in place in Canada, Germany, Sweden and France. Just to the north of us, Canadian citizens are fined and sometimes jailed for publicly criticizing the homosexual establishment.

In Belgium, a bill has been introduced that would forbid anyone from being a member of an organization (secular or religious) that "differentiates between people on the basis of their sexual conduct or relational preference." If this law is passed, or others like it that have been introduced in other Western countries, homosexuals will be able to prosecute any priest, minister or religious teacher who instructs his congregation in the teachings of the Bible on homosexuality.

PUNISHMENT FOR "HOMOPHOBIA"?

Most Americans are still unaware of the homosexual lobby's power to make even well-respected organizations beg, apologize and cave in to demands. Stories like the following are happening all around the country. Early in 1996, in San Francisco, when a group of homosexuals attempted to intrude into policy making at the Salvation Army, the organization issued a statement claiming that homosexuality presents "a serious threat to the integrity, quality and solidarity of society as a whole."

Salvation Army officials had not counted on the city's Board of Supervisors holding up a federal grant of $65,000, as punishment for their "homophobia." Unprepared to take the loss of money, officers of the Salvation Army fell into line, as many before and since have been forced to do. Gritting their teeth, they not only pledged to change their policies concerning "gays," but also set up "sensitivity" sessions to indoctrinate staff members into correct thinking on the subject.

HOMOSEXUALITY AS "ETHNICITY"

[The] conception of gay people as a new kind of ethnic group is the central pillar of gay-rights mythology; it is what unites [authors] Bruce Bawer and Michelangelo Signorile, Act-Up [AIDS Coalition to Unleash Power] and the gay Republicans. With the growth of the gay subculture as a commercial and ideological enterprise, the subjective feeling that being homosexual was almost like being a member of a race hardened into a political dogma. Against the fact that homosexuality is a behavior and not a trait such as blue eyes or red hair, the ideologues of the gay movement had to construct a single overarching concept that would unify a great many diverse individuals. What they came up with was the idea of homosexuality as an intrinsic quality, not a behavior but a state of being, and more than that—an inheritable characteristic, genetically inscribed in every cell. Strangely, these very same people scream bloody murder whenever anyone attributes the behavior of other victim groups, such as women or blacks, to genetic factors.

Justin Raimondo, Insight, September 12, 1994.

At a Denver hospital, the government mandated that "sensitivity" sessions be held to re-educate its staff on homosexuality. All employees were instructed to wear buttons saying, "It's Okay to be Gay," pinned to their clothing. Those employees who refused were publicly humiliated for their stubbornness.

At Denver's Metro State College, the Civil Rights Commission threatened to shut down a religious Jewish student group if it refused to accept openly homosexual members. It may soon be that a group's refusal to alter its membership requirements will constitute a "hate crime" and carry a jail term.

Along with feminists, homosexuals are now close to dominating all the power centers of our society. It is because of the vast power they have accumulated that they now feel confident to make their preposterous demand for same-sex "marriage." However many times the demand to legalize their "partner-ships" is defeated, the homosexual lobby will return to resurrect it—until such a law is passed.

Thanks to the media, American society is now being bathed, if not drowned, in homosexual propaganda. From television sit-coms and soap operas to movies and daily newspaper features, we are awash in the ethos of "gayness." Outright, even fervent approval of homosexual behavior is now a litmus test demanded from all straights.

Dr. Charles Socarides, a founder of NARTH, writes, "Movies have been routinely censored by a gay Hollywood review board for the last seven to eight years; other films critical of homosex-uality have been boycotted at the box office; books which por-tray homosexuality in any unfavorable way have not been pub-lished, and many such books have been removed from library shelves in universities and public libraries."

Describing what he calls "heavily political and polemical" literature on homosexuality, psychiatrist Joseph Berger says, "Because most people do not have a detailed knowledge of the scientific literature on homosexuality, they are vulnerable to the vast amount of incorrect and often deliberately misleading information that receives disproportionate publicity in the media." Dr. Berger warns the ordinary reader not to give in unthinkingly to what is "one of the most powerful propaganda exercises of modern times.". . .

AMERICANS MUST COME TO THEIR SENSES

There is now a slow but growing movement of "covenant" set-tlements, where like-minded people are coming together to form their own communities. These are not communes by any means, but resemble more the neighborhoods of orthodox reli-gious groups, whose members buy land and houses and rent contiguous buildings in a given region, in order to be assured of neighbors who share their values and desire the same whole-some environment for their children.

Unfortunately, we may also be faced with an expansion of more militant militia and patriot groups, as people throw up their hands in exasperation over what they perceive as an inabil-ity to escape an invasive, morally deteriorating culture. Syndi-cated columnist Walter Williams writes that most militia mem-bers are good, conscientious citizens, who are growing fearful of the arbitrary nature of government. He says, "What distinguishes them, misguided or not, is a willingness to prepare to resist a government seemingly hell-bent on making a mockery of our constitutional guarantees."

We can only hope that before there is any serious conflict, Americans will come to their senses and cease granting, through indifference and default, political power to this country's internal enemies. Critical choices will have to be made. It's up to us to decide if we're ready to discard the wisdom of the ages, or if we have the will to maintain the sanctions and taboos that have prevailed in and sustained all societies.

"The time has come for America to recognize that lesbians, gay men and bisexuals should be protected from discrimination in the workplace, in housing and in public accommodations."

HOMOSEXUALS NEED ANTIDISCRIMINATION LAWS

American Civil Liberties Union

The American Civil Liberties Union (ACLU) is a national organization that works to defend Americans' civil rights guaranteed by the U.S. Constitution. In the following viewpoint, the ACLU maintains that gay people are often denied jobs, promotions, and housing because of prejudice against their sexual orientation. To combat this discrimination, the ACLU advocates laws to protect the civil rights of gays and lesbians. Specifically, the authors call for the enactment of the proposed Employment Non-Discrimination Act (ENDA), which would prohibit employment discrimination on the basis of sexual orientation. Passing such legislation, the authors contend, would be a modest but essential first step in securing equal rights for gays and lesbians. As of December 1998, Congress had not passed ENDA.

As you read, consider the following questions:

1. According to the *Wall Street Journal* poll cited by the ACLU, what percentage of Fortune 500 executives would hesitate to promote a homosexual?
2. How do most gays and lesbians try to avoid workplace discrimination, according to the authors?

Reprinted from the ACLU's testimony on the Employment Non-Discrimination Act—H.R. 1863 before the Subcommittee on Government Programs, Committee on Small Business, U.S. House of Representatives, July 17, 1996.

The American Civil Liberties Union is a nationwide, nonpartisan organization dedicated to defending the principles embodied in the Constitution and the Bill of Rights. The organization began in 1920 and today is 270,000 members strong.

The American Civil Liberties Union supports the Employment Non-Discrimination Act (ENDA). We believe that in America, the ability to get and keep a job should depend on ability and willingness to work. The basic governing principle ought to be merit, and that same principle should govern housing and service in public accommodations. Over the last fifty years, we as a society have recognized that sometimes the merit system does not work, that some Americans are denied employment, housing and service for reasons that are arbitrary and unfair, reasons like race, religion and gender. When that happens, our response has been to pass laws aimed at restoring the merit system by making sure that arbitrary considerations do not govern access to employment, housing and public accommodations. These laws, we believe, are an essential component of making the 14th Amendment's promise of equal protection of the law real.

The time has come for America to recognize that lesbians, gay men and bisexuals should be protected from discrimination in the workplace, in housing and in public accommodations. ENDA is an important, but in some ways modest, step in that direction. Congress should pass it without delay.

THE CASE FOR CIVIL RIGHTS PROTECTION

Although all arbitrary discrimination is wrong, workplace discrimination is especially egregious. In most circumstances in America today, employment is essential to any kind of a decent life, and it can be essential to survival. To deprive anyone of employment is to deprive them of sustenance.

Congress knows how pervasive employment discrimination against gays and lesbians has been and is. And case studies about how many gay men and lesbians have lost or been denied jobs or promotions vastly understate the problem. The threat of discrimination is a very real presence in most American workplaces. For example, a 1987 *Wall Street Journal* poll of Fortune 500 executives showed 66% would hesitate to give a management job to a lesbian or a gay man. Most gay men and lesbians attempt to protect themselves against the threat of discrimination by hiding their identity. But hiding one's identity is no simple task. It requires carefully policing even the most casual conversations, and banishing almost any acknowledgment of family and friends from the workplace (those who doubt it should try to see how far they can get through a single day without referring to a spouse or companion). In addition to being difficult to do, hiding one's identity is harmful; it hurts the workplace, building walls between co-workers, and it can impose a terrible psychological toll on those forced to do the hiding.

It also appears from the best evidence available today that employment discrimination takes a toll at the most basic level: income. Although opponents of civil rights claim that lesbians and gay men are well heeled, the only thing close to a representative survey suggests that lesbians and gay men generally earn less than their heterosexual counterparts.

And it is plain today beyond any doubt that discrimination against lesbians and gay men in the workplace is arbitrary. Claims that lesbians and gay men are mentally ill or that they harm the efficiency of the workplace have been shown up as baseless myths. And as Congress discovered in 1994, the evidence is now overwhelming that even in the context of the military, lesbians and gay men are every bit as capable as heterosexuals.

Finally, popular belief to the contrary, lesbians and gay men are not protected by civil rights laws in most of the United States. Only nine states comprehensively prohibit employment discrimination. Courts have consistently ruled that sexual orientation is not covered under Title VII of the 1964 Civil Rights Act.

WHAT ENDA WOULD DO

ENDA would ban discrimination based on sexual orientation in all aspects of employment, including hiring, firing, promotion, compensation, and most terms and conditions of employment. Sexual orientation could no longer be a basis for employment decisions. ENDA's ban on discrimination will protect heterosexuals as well as lesbians and gay men, and it will protect workers who associate with gay and lesbian co-workers. It will also protect workers who support it from retaliation.

But as noted above, ENDA is modest. It applies only to discrimination in employment, not to housing and public accommodations, and only to employers with 15 or more employees. ENDA explicitly does not require that fringe benefits be provided to the partners of lesbian and gay workers. ENDA explicitly forbids the uses of quotas or preferential treatment of any kind, and it explicitly does not permit "disparate impact" claims. [Disparate impact is "intentional discrimination"—when an employer deliberately treats an employee differently because of his or her minority group status.] ENDA does not apply to service in the armed forces and it will have no effect on veterans' preference programs. ENDA does not apply to religious organizations except to the extent that they engage in commercial businesses so divorced from their religious functions that they are subject to federal income taxes. The exemption explicitly includes religious schools and hospitals.

In its basic structure, ENDA parallels Title VII of the 1964 Civil Rights Act, the law which prohibits employment discrimination based on race, religion and gender. It provides exactly the same procedures and remedies that Title VII provides.

EQUAL RIGHTS ARE NOT "SPECIAL RIGHTS"

ENDA forbids employment discrimination based on sexual orientation, nothing more and nothing less. As the Supreme Court observed in *Evans v. Romer*, anti-discrimination laws are not "special rights." To most of us, the right to have and keep a job, as the court observed, is taken for granted, either because we are already protected against discrimination or because we do not face discrimination. But to those who do face discrimination, there is nothing "special" about a law aimed at preserving your ability to work—the most essential aspect of ordinary day to day life in America.

Reprinted by permission of Kirk Anderson.

The claim that lesbians and gay men as a group represent a threat to children is untrue, as is the claim that lesbians and gay men have negative effects on children when they are parents or function as role models, and those who make those arguments have no respectable scientific support whatsoever.

Finally, the argument that we should deny civil rights protection to lesbians and gay men to discourage people from being gay is ridiculous. Whatever the sources of sexual orientation may be, it is very clear that is not a casual choice, subject to simple change in the face of government incentive. More important, in workplace terms there simply is nothing wrong with being gay. Lesbians and gay men are capable, neither better nor worse as employees. In a pluralistic society in which work is essential to survival, we can not allow one person's opinions about the worth, job performance aside, of another to determine if that other person is able to work. Perhaps even more important, in that kind of pluralistic society, we should not use discrimination in the workplace to try to change the most fundamental aspects of people's lives. That is why we ban discrimination based on religion, and why we ban most forms of marital status discrimination as well.

PUTTING AN END TO DISCRIMINATION

ENDA enjoys broad-based support. Poll after poll has shown that the majority of Americans feel that gays and lesbians should have protection from employment discrimination. A recent *Newsweek* poll showed that 84% of the American public supports ending workplace discrimination against gay men and lesbians. ENDA has been endorsed by the Leadership Conference on Civil Rights and is one of LCCR's legislative priorities for the 104th Congress. In addition, major corporations—AT&T, Eastman Kodak, Microsoft, RJR Nabisco, Quaker Oats, and Xerox—specifically endorse ENDA. Numerous religious groups also support ENDA: National Council of Churches, National Catholic Conference for Interracial Justice, Southern Christian Leadership Conference, and the Union of American Hebrew Congregations.

At one time, most of America accepted employment discrimination based on race and gender. Both were justified "pragmatically"—with common wisdom, later proved false, that women and African Americans, for example, were not able employees. Both were also justified "morally"—with the pious certainty that Italians and Irish, for example, were morally inferior and that god had ordained that women not work outside the home. Many Americans still hold such views, but we look back at the days when those views held sway in the workplace with shame and embarrassment.

It is as plain as it could be that in the not too distant future, we will look back with shame and embarrassment at an era in which discrimination against lesbians, gay men and bisexuals was justified with myths about gay people and the certainty that god approved. Leaders should lead. It is time for Congress to begin the process of putting an end to discrimination based on sexual orientation.

"Homosexual 'rights' are not about equality under the law, which homosexuals already possess, but about special privileges and legitimization of their lifestyle."

HOMOSEXUALS DO NOT NEED ANTIDISCRIMINATION LAWS

Concerned Women for America

In the following viewpoint, Concerned Women for America (CWA) argues that homosexuals do not need antidiscrimination laws. According to CWA, homosexuals as a group have not exhibited an inability to obtain income, education, or political power because of societal prejudice against their sexual orientation. For this reason, the authors argue against the proposed Employment Non-Discrimination Act (ENDA), which would include homosexuals as a protected group under employment discrimination laws. Such legislation is unnecessary because homosexuals do not meet the criteria for minority class status, CWA contends. Moreover, the authors assert, ENDA would require employers to knowingly hire homosexuals, thereby infringing on the rights of businesses that support traditional moral beliefs. CWA is a national organization that promotes traditional Judeo-Christian values.

As you read, consider the following questions:

1. According to CWA, what are the three standards that determine protected class status?
2. According to Simmons Market Research Bureau, cited by CWA, what is the average household income of homosexuals?

Abridged from the Concerned Women for America policy paper "The Big Bad Wolf in Sheep's Clothing: The Employment Non-Discrimination Act," November 1997. Reprinted with permission.

Skin color is a benign, non-behavioral characteristic. Sexual orientation is perhaps the most profound of human behavioral characteristics. Comparison of the two is a convenient but invalid argument.

—General Colin Powell

T he Employment Non-Discrimination Act of 1997 was introduced on June 10th in the 105th Congress by Senator Jim Jeffords (R-VT). The purpose of ENDA is to include "sexual orientation" as a protected class under employment discrimination laws. But ENDA is really bad business. It grants homosexuals the benefits of minority class status—based solely upon their behavior.

HUMBLE BEGINNINGS

Over the past several years, the homosexual movement has been phenomenally successful in advancing its public policy and legislative agenda. This success began in earnest when the American Psychological Association (APA) officially dropped the inclusion of homosexuality as a disorder in 1973 in the 3rd edition of the *Diagnostic and Statistical Manual* (DSM-III). Since then, the homosexual agenda has permeated every aspect of society, including your workplace and the education of your children. By using humor and sympathy, they have carefully manipulated the minds and hearts of Americans into believing their lifestyle is normal. One has only to look at the television show *Ellen* and the many homosexual characters on other shows to see the homosexual invasion. The ENDA bill continues this assault by injecting the homosexual morality into a civil rights debate. Its ultimate goal is to have society accept their lifestyle choice as "normal."

In 1995, homosexual activists attempted to redefine marriage to include same-sex partners in Hawaii. Because of the "full faith and credit" clause of the Constitution, these "marriages" would have had to have been recognized by each state in the union. Continuing this trend on the federal level, the homosexual community is attempting to force societal acceptance from a different slant: workplace discrimination. Voters in Washington state rejected one attempt of equal protection, but the homosexual community is always working on several fronts. In order to garner support, they draw on sympathetic, fair-minded Americans and members of Congress who would never tolerate an unfair form of discrimination. Their rhetoric has highjacked the civil rights movement. Like in Washington state, the homosexual community claims they are not seeking special rights, only equal protection under the law.

In 1996, the Supreme Court ruled that Colorado's Amendment 2 was unconstitutional in *Romer v. Evans*. [Amendment 2 was a ballot initiative that attempted to bar legal claims of discrimination by homosexuals.] The Supreme Court found that homosexuals who were discriminated against were not seeking "special rights." The Court wrote, "we find nothing special in the protections Amendment 2 withholds. These are protections taken for granted by most people, either because they already have them or do not need them." As a result, the homosexual community has used this decision as a building block for federal legislation.

A NECESSARY LAW?

Historically, protected class status is determined by the courts and civil rights authorities by three standards. They are:

1. *As an entire class, they exhibit obvious, immutable, or distinguishing characteristics, such as race, color, gender, or national origin, that define them as a discrete group.*

Essentially, homosexuals, bisexuals and lesbians, by their own admission, share only one attribute on which they base their claim to protected class status: They choose to perform sexual acts with members of the same gender. Behavior alone is not a compelling reason to reward protected, minority, or ethnic class status with all the attendant entitlements.

2. *As an entire class, they have suffered a history of discrimination evidenced by lack of ability to obtain economic income, adequate education, or cultural opportunity.*

Homosexuals are enormously advantaged relative to the general population. According to the Institute for International Research in New York City, a survey conducted by Simmons Market Research Bureau claims that homosexuals have an average household income of $63,100.00 versus a general population income of $36,500.00. By contrast, the average income of a disadvantaged African-American household is somewhere between $12–13,000.

In fact, homosexuals do far better financially than most American families. According to Overlooked Opinions, a homosexual polling firm, the annual income of homosexual households is 41 percent higher than the national average. In addition, nearly half of all gay households include someone holding a professional/managerial job. And *Businessweek* noted that homosexuals are five times more likely than the average American to earn $100,000 a year.

3. *As an entire class, they clearly demonstrate political powerlessness.*

During the 1996 elections, the Humans Rights Campaign Fund, a homosexual political advocacy group, raised more than $1.4 million. This put it in the top 1 percent of political action committees (PAC's) nationwide.

To further illustrate the point that homosexuals as a class are not politically powerless, Vice President Al Gore wrote in a letter to a member of Concerned Women for America (CWA):

> This Administration has taken more steps than any previous to bring the gay and lesbian communities to the table. We have more openly gay and lesbian individuals serving in appointed positions, and their impact—through both their expertise and their efforts to advocate for the concerns of gay and lesbian Americans—has been significant.

In November of 1997, President Bill Clinton agreed to give the keynote speech at the Human Rights Campaign fundraising dinner. This was more than the rubber chicken fundraising circuit, however. He is the first president to address a homosexual advocacy group. Leaders of the homosexual movement say that by speaking at this dinner, President Clinton recognized the power of the homosexual vote and *validated* its civil rights issues—one of which is the ENDA bill. President Clinton's remarks at the dinner included calling for a redefinition "of the immutable ideals that have guided us from the beginning" to include acceptance of gays and lesbians. With this kind of exposure, it is difficult to validate a claim of political powerlessness.

HOMOSEXUALS AS A PROTECTED CLASS?

In other words, homosexuals are upwardly mobile, politically powerful citizens who have chosen to involve themselves in sexual behavior that is neither inborn nor unchangeable. Now, they are clamoring for protected class status—special legal standing and advantages historically applied by governments in the United States to classes of people sharing distinct and immutable characteristics.

Homosexuals are not a model of a disadvantaged minority class. Disregarding the standard gay rights rhetoric, their movement is nothing more than a powerful special interest lobby intent on using their money and political influence to "piggyback" on legitimate gains of the truly disadvantaged. They can only gain these special rights and privileges at the expense of others.

Homosexual "rights" are not about equality under the law, which homosexuals already possess, but about *special privileges* and legitimization of their lifestyle. Clamoring for this protected status borders on the ridiculous when seen in the bright light of logic.

Addressing the homosexual community's claims of discrimination in the workplace, the National Gay and Lesbian Task Force Policy Institute released a report entitled "Pervasive Patterns of Discrimination." In this report, they cited the results of 21 surveys of homosexuals over 11 years and concluded there were 1,583 cases of workplace discrimination based on one's sexual orientation. But what they didn't report was that assuming the survey was unbiased, sexual orientation discrimination suits accounted for less than 1% of the discrimination charges reported to the Equal Employment Opportunity Commission. The question then must be raised, how was the discrimination determined? Did a homosexual man declare he was discriminated against because of his sexual orientation when in actuality he was the least qualified for a promotion?

DISCRIMINATION COMPLEXITIES

Current law allows special protection in employment for people based on their race, age, and gender. These are immutable characteristics. Alveda King, the niece of Martin Luther King, Jr. and a civil rights activist, describes it this way:

> I used to be very overweight. When I was large, I could have chosen to be a victim, like many other obese people, and lobbied for laws protecting obese people from discrimination, but I decided to make a change. That's what we're facing today in the debate over homosexual rights. Homosexuals can either choose to be victims, or choose to make a change.

Sexual orientation is a *behavior* that can change. ENDA would be granting protected status to a group of people who exhibit one particular behavior. By that same logic, any group identified by a specific behavior could be eligible for special protected class status—from vegetarians to drug abusers. ENDA would prohibit an employer from making a decision regarding an employee (hiring, firing, promotion, etc.) based on his or her sexual orientation, even if homosexuality is against the employer's moral or religious beliefs.

U.S. businesses are already struggling under the heavy burden of excessive government regulations. Adding sexual orientation to the list of protected classes would place an even greater burden on businesses by allowing the federal government to scrutinize another dimension of employer hiring and firing practices.

ENDA forbids employers from adopting quotas or giving preferential treatment based on sexual orientation. However, adding sexual orientation to the list of groups that qualify for special protected class status would have far reaching implications when it comes to proving that one is *not* discriminating against homosexuals. An employer would no doubt keep records of his homosexual employees in order to "prove" that he *is* hiring homosexuals.

Reprinted by permission of Chuck Asay and Creators Syndicate.

Additionally, ENDA would burst open the floodgates of litigation. If civil rights protection is broadened to include changeable behaviors, employers would be put in the difficult position of evaluating "sexual orientation." When a black or Hispanic person interviews, the employer knows from their appearance that they belong to a special protected class. How is a business supposed to know if a prospective employee is a homosexual? And, what would prevent a person from claiming he was gay in order to be hired because of some government imposed quota?

Would an employer have to ask every person he interviewed if they preferred to have someone of the opposite sex or the same sex as a sexual partner? They wouldn't be able to do this for fear of provoking a lawsuit similar to lawsuits asking a person's age or marital status. However, if they don't ask, how will they know they are not vulnerable to later claims of "discrimination"? A disgruntled former employee could falsely claim to be a homosexual in order to file an unlimited damages suit. This is lose-lose legislation. . . .

The Devil Is in the Details

Although churches and religious schools are exempt from ENDA, their for profit entities (with 15 or more employees) would *not* be exempted from ENDA. This means that Christian bookstores, day-care centers, summer camps, and radio stations with 15 or more employees must comply with ENDA. Non-profit organizations would also be subject to ENDA—which means Christian-based non-profit organizations or religious political groups would have to adhere to this law. Ultimately, an employer with moral or religious beliefs against homosexuality would be forced to lay down their own rights at the altar of the federal government.

ENDA would also cover federal employees generally, including employees of Congress and presidential appointees.

ENDA's extension of special rights to homosexuals would affect all public employers, from the federal level all the way down to small city governments. Local police forces could be subject to homosexual hiring quotas, mandated recruitment of homosexuals, and "sensitivity training" for police officers. . . .

Overall, ENDA would be bad for businesses, bad for government, and certainly bad for Americans who do not sanction homosexual behavior. Homosexual activists are engaged in a campaign of misinformation and lies. They are demanding special privileges instead of legitimate rights. They are gently tugging at the sympathies of the average American as well as the unsuspecting member of Congress in order to gain more political power.

"To the detriment of many gay teens,
their peers, parents, teachers, and
counselors have failed to recognize
the connections between homophobia
and the suicide risks for gay youth."

HOMOPHOBIA INCREASES THE SUICIDE RISK FOR GAY TEENS

Frances Snowder

Gay teens are at increased risk for suicide because of society's aversion to homosexuality, argues Frances Snowder in the following viewpoint. She maintains that adolescence is an especially vulnerable time for gay youths because they receive little or no emotional support as they try to come to terms with their sexuality. In fact, Snowder contends, many gay teens encounter antigay verbal and physical abuse in schools and at home, which increases the chances that they will engage in self-destructive behaviors. Furthermore, she points out, teachers and school counselors often exacerbate the problem by harboring negative attitudes about homosexuality. To help prevent gay teen suicide, educators must develop gay-supportive school environments, Snowder concludes. Snowder is a former high school and college teacher who lives in Columbia, Maryland.

As you read, consider the following questions:

1. What percentage of youth suicides are committed by gay teens, according to Snowder?
2. In the author's opinion, why is it difficult to obtain accurate data on homosexuality?

Reprinted from Frances Snowder, "Preventing Gay Teen Suicide," in *Open Lives, Safe Schools*, edited by Donovan R. Walling (Bloomington, IN: Phi Delta Kappa Educational Foundation, 1996), by permission of the publisher. *References in the original have been omitted in this reprint.*

Gay* youth are most at risk of suicide during the critical adolescent years when they are attempting to explore their own identities and to form adult emotional relationships. This is a time when they need the most support from family, peers, and others. Unfortunately, many gay youth do not find such support in their homes or schools.

Gay teens represent a significant percentage of the adolescents who commit or attempt suicide. Approximately 500,000 adolescents attempt suicide every year. Recent reports confirm that more than 5,000 succeed, and at least 30% of completed suicides (or some 1,500 each year) are gay youth. In addition, gay youth are two to six times more likely to attempt suicide than heterosexual youth.

Many homeless children are on the streets because they have run away or been cast out of their homes because of conflicts over their sexual orientation. Youth in schools who remain anonymous and silent often have been frightened into emotional isolation by the prevalent homophobic environment. They often choose not to confide in authority figures, such as teachers and counselors, whom they fear will diminish or disregard their feelings; expose them to embarrassment, ridicule, or harassment; or try to "cure" them.

Unfortunately, the concerns of gay teens are not adequately addressed in the literature for teachers, school administrators, health providers, and guidance counselors. In fact, until recent years, the numerous studies done on adolescents and suicide failed even to mention gay youth.

RESEARCH ON GAY TEEN SUICIDE

Although pioneering research on gay teen suicide was done by physicians Ronald F.C. Kourany and Gary Remafedi as early as the mid-1980s, the national alert in the United States was not sounded until 1989 by Paul Gibson's ground-breaking article, "Gay Male and Lesbian Youth Suicide" in *Report of the Secretary's Task Force on Youth Suicide*, published by the U.S. Department of Health and Human Services. This controversial report to the Bush Administration first stated that gay teens account for 30% of all youth suicides.

Unfortunately, questions about the reliability of the report's statistics superseded any positive political action. However, the 30% statistic holds fast in a 1994 book, *Death by Denial: Studies of Suicide in Gay and Lesbian Teenagers*, edited by Gary Remafedi. An an-

---

*In the context of this essay, "gay" is an inclusive term comprising all sexual minorities: homosexual males, lesbians, and bisexual and transsexual individuals.

thology of the major research on the subject, Remafedi's book republishes his own 1991 article along with Kourany's 1987 article, "Suicide Among Homosexual Adolescents," and the Gibson report. Though far from comprehensive, this book, which contains only four other major research articles and the text of the state legislation passed by the Governor's Commission on Gay and Lesbian Youth in Massachusetts, is regarded as the most authoritative text on the subject to date.

Of the included studies, most deal exclusively with gay and bisexual males. Those studies that include all of the various sexual minorities as a total group tend to slight the issues for lesbians and transsexual youth and omit the effects of various gender proscriptions in racial and ethnic minority cultures. The fact that most of the articles now are several years old also indicates that sexual minority suicide is a subject that requires much more serious scholarly attention.

However, a major problem with researching matters pertaining to teen sexual orientation is the lack of reliable information. It is virtually impossible at this time to get fully truthful and accurate data on homosexuality, because the subject is so stigmatized and access to the underage teen population is difficult to obtain. Most statistics on teen sexual orientation are based on surveys that ask respondents to self-report.

In addition to a lack of dependable research data on gay teens in general, other factors obstruct the collection of data on gay teen suicide. Data on suicide is collected in different ways from various states and even from counties within states. Cultural taboos against suicide and homosexuality also tend to result in the under-reporting of gay suicides. Families may conceal information, for example, reporting suicides as accidents.

Cultural norms also may obscure teen suicide issues. For example, researcher Joyce Hunter quotes H.F. Myers, who reports, "Black gay youths may be more inclined to provoke others to kill them rather than to commit suicide; such victim-precipitated homicide may mask the frequency of suicide in this group."

Known Risk Factors

Certainly, further research is necessary to help educators fully understand these matters, but today's teachers and administrators can deal with what already is known. For example, in "Risk Factors for Attempted Suicide in Gay and Bisexual Youth," Gary Remafedi, James Farrow, and Robert Deisher contend that most gay youth suicides are committed by teens dealing for the first time with issues of sexual orientation and identity. In this 1991 study of attempted suicide survivors who subsequently identified themselves as gay, the authors reported that "almost one-third of subjects made their first suicide attempt in the same year that they identified themselves as bisexual or homosexual. Overall, three-fourths of all first attempts temporally followed self-labeling."

HOMOSEXUALITY AND SUICIDE

A connection between suicide and homosexuality has long been recognized in the popular culture, reflected in music (e.g., "The Ode to Billie Joe"), movies (e.g., *The Boys in the Band*), theater (e.g., Lillian Hellman's *The Children's Hour*), and other art forms. Yet, few researchers have ventured to explore the link between sexual orientation and self-injury. Early evidence of an association appeared as incidental findings in studies of adult sexuality. They revealed that gay men were much more likely to have attempted suicide than heterosexual men and that their attempts often occurred during adolescence. Newer studies have provided consistent evidence of unusually high rates of attempted suicide among gay youth, in the range of 20–30 percent, regardless of geographic and ethnic variability.

Gary Remafedi, *Death by Denial: Studies of Suicide in Gay and Lesbian Teenagers*, 1994.

Although declassified as a psychopathologic illness in 1973 by the American Psychiatric Association, homosexuality often is still treated as an abnormality in many clinical settings. This situation led the American Medical Association to repudiate "reparative" therapy in 1994, calling instead for a "non-judgmental recognition of sexual orientation" by physicians. For school people, this evolving attitude should signal an awareness that, unlike other troubled adolescents who are at-risk for suicide, gay teens may be psychologically healthy; but gay teens must cope with a gay-hostile environment that, if internalized, can be destructive to self-esteem—and survival.

VERBAL AND PHYSICAL ABUSE

Hostility may be physical as well as psychological. Fear and hatred of gay and lesbian youth are acted out in name-calling and physical abuse. Verbal and physical abuse most often occur at home and in school, both places where most teenagers might expect to be protected and to feel safe. In a 1992 study conducted by the National Gay and Lesbian Task Force, 45% of the gay men and 20% of the lesbians surveyed had been victims of verbal and physical assaults in secondary school because of their sexual orientation.

Another study of 500 New York City youths served by a gay youth services agency revealed that 46% of those who had experienced a violent physical attack reported that the assault was gay-related. Of those who had experienced violence in their homes, 61% reported the abuse as gay-related.

In 1993 the Massachusetts Governor's Commission on Gay and Lesbian Youth reported a study that surveyed 218 adolescents at seven community-based gay and lesbian youth groups and eight school-based gay/straight alliances across Massachusetts. The responses to four of the 33 survey questions are noteworthy. (Category totals may not equal 100% because of rounding.)

"How would most students in your high school react to finding out a student they knew was lesbian, gay, or bisexual?"

Negative	60%
Neutral	21%
Mixed	13%
Positive	5%

"How would the parents of most of your friends react to finding out that their child was lesbian, gay, or bisexual?"

Negative	60%
Neutral	17%
Positive	17%
Mixed	7%

"Have you ever heard teachers in your high school make anti-lesbian or anti-gay remarks?"

Yes	53%
No	47%

"How often do you hear anti-gay or anti-lesbian remarks made at your high school?"

Sometimes	51%
Often	43%
Never	6%

Ritch C. Savin-Williams' 1994 research on verbal and physical abuse as stressors in the lives of lesbians, gay males, and bisexual youths associates substance abuse, promiscuity, alcoholism, running away, and delinquency among gay teens with crises over sexual orientation. And, as would be expected, Savin-Williams found a strong correlation between such self-destructive behavior patterns and suicide attempts.

To the detriment of many gay teens, their peers, parents, teachers, and counselors have failed to recognize the connections between homophobia and the suicide risks for gay youth. Diane

Allensworth, speaking as associate executive director for programs for the American School Health Association, stated that a recent survey of its members who are school nurses and health teachers revealed that "homosexuality was the number one topic they weren't equipped to discuss."

Similarly, a study of 289 secondary school counselors published in the December 1991 *Journal of School Health* reported that "17% thought there were no gay students in their school and 20% thought they would not be competent counseling gay students."

James T. Sears, an associate professor of education at South Carolina University, has used a number of psychological instruments to document the highly negative attitudes toward gays of students, teachers, prospective teachers, and guidance counselors in the schools. For example, a survey of prospective teachers and existing counselors found that "eight out of ten prospective teachers harbored negative feeling towards lesbians and gay men. One-third were classified as 'high grade homophobics.' Two-thirds of existing counselors expressed negative attitudes and feelings about homosexuality and less than one-quarter have chosen to counsel homosexual students."

REDUCING THE RISKS

If gay youth are allowed to be themselves and the issues of gay teens are adequately addressed by teachers, guidance counselors, and health workers, many suicides can be prevented. The necessity of leading a stigmatized and sometimes double life is a heavy burden for an adult. It is even heavier for an adolescent first coming to terms with issues of identity and sexuality. Without role models, without support from friends and family, gay teenagers often are unable to complete the critical transition to adulthood. Suicide, at that low point, is considered a way out. And now a terrible new trend has been identified: purposely contracting AIDS.

How, then, can educators reduce the risks to gay youth? Following are three basic suggestions:

First, nondiscrimination policies regarding sexual orientation would aid in suicide prevention efforts in the schools. Such policies would prohibit teachers, students, and others from verbally or physically harassing gay students (or colleagues). If such policies were publicized and enforced, they would inspire trust and boost the self-esteem of gay students.

When school policies set the tone for a gay-supportive school environment and resources are available to gay students, students who are anxious or questioning about their sexual orientation will be more likely to seek the help of teachers and counselors. However, when gay students go to their teachers and counselors with their problems, those professionals need to be adequately informed about the issues and in a position to help.

Thus a second suggestion is in order: Proactive schools will need to devote time and money to staff development. Schools that adopt a proactive stance on gay youth issues also may wish to seek out openly gay educators and other professionals to lead workshops and seminars. If the limitations of regional politics prohibit such a direct approach, then school leaders, at the very least, can provide professional literature on gay issues and access for teachers and counselors to seminars and other forms of training at regional and national conferences or through university classes.

Third, schools should provide "safe" options for students to learn about their sexuality and to discuss sexual orientation issues. Many youth in distress over sexual orientation and identity do not wish to "come out of the closet" to individuals in their school, no matter how accepting the school environment is. Therefore, indirect approaches also should be developed, such as providing information brochures in the library or counseling center. Resource addresses and telephone hotline numbers can be posted on easily accessible bulletin boards. A selection of gay fiction and nonfiction books can be maintained openly in the school library. Gay-affirmative literature and services should be provided in schools so that the legitimate issues of gay youth can be discussed openly.

These efforts will help to make discussions and information about sexual issues a normal part of the learning process. Sexual awareness and self-knowledge and identity are part of living—and should be part of learning. When the subject of homosexuality is normalized by and for educators and other service providers, public opinion will change and homophobia can be reduced. Then teens, who once would have struggled to understand their sexual identity alone and in fear, will be able to find accurate information, sympathetic understanding, and simple acceptance from educators they trust and respect. Such an environment will help to maintain and enhance healthy self-esteem, and gay teens will no longer be at risk of suicide.

| "Gay teen suicide is an outright
  myth."

THE PROBLEM OF GAY TEEN SUICIDE HAS BEEN EXAGGERATED

Philip Jenkins

In the following viewpoint, Philip Jenkins argues that gay rights activists rely on skewed statistics on the percentage of homosexuals in the population, causing them to overstate the suicide risk for gay teens. The popular belief that homosexuals comprise 10 percent of the population is based on a 1940s study by Alfred Kinsey, Jenkins points out. This study, he maintains, has been disproved by more recent evidence revealing that only 2 to 3 percent of the population is homosexual. However, Jenkins contends, Kinsey's statistics are still the basis for estimates on the number of suicides committed by gay teens. Gay rights supporters then use these exaggerated estimates to promote their political agenda, he concludes. Jenkins is the head of the religious studies program at Pennsylvania State University in University Park. He is also the author of *Pedophiles and Priests: Anatomy of a Social Crisis*.

As you read, consider the following questions:

1. According to the 1994 University of Chicago study cited by Jenkins, what percentage of women identify themselves as homosexual or bisexual?
2. What percentage of men are exclusively homosexual, according to the author?
3. In Jenkins's opinion, why is Paul Gibson not a reputable source for current estimates on the number of gay teen suicides?

Excerpted from Philip Jenkins, "One in Ten: A Gay Mythology," *Chronicles: A Magazine of American Culture*, October 1996. Reprinted by permission of the author.

Gay issues are likely to remain central to social and political debate in this country for many years to come, whether in the form of gay rights referenda, gay service in the military, school curricula, or the adoption of children by homosexual couples. It should not be too long before one specific issue, the recognition of gay marriage by federal law, ignites a legal and constitutional crisis. Such controversies usually involve a familiar range of principles and rhetorical styles, above all the confrontation of moralistic and libertarian approaches, and a fundamental difference over the rights of the "consenting adult" versus the traditional social consensus. However, to a startling extent, both supporters and opponents of gay rights tend to accept as factual certain ideas about the nature and prevalence of homosexual behavior, notions which in reality range from the dubious to the downright bogus. Based on incorrect assumptions and misleading research, a whole mythology has attained general credence in academe and the media, with profound consequences for the ongoing social debate. This is no case of conspiracy theory, as the exponents of this fiction are overwhelmingly guilty of optimistic self-deception rather than any more calculated motives; yet the results are more effective than could have been imagined by the most Machiavellian schemer. The rarely challenged assertion that homosexuals represent "one in ten" of the population has proved a rhetorical weapon of immense force.

THE "TEN PERCENT" THEORY

Different societies accept different forms of argument as providing confirmation for a given statement. While the ultimate warrant was once the scriptural text, the knockout blow in a controversy today is normally delivered in the form of a social science statistic, proving that some inconceivably vast proportion of the population is subject to ills like child abuse, domestic violence, or ethnic intimidation, each of which must therefore be treated as an "epidemic" in need of countermeasures. These figures are most likely to develop a cultural life of their own if they come in some easily memorable form, preferably incorporating a pleasingly round number like "fifty thousand" or "three million." Perhaps the best-known of these killer statistics is the estimate for the number of homosexuals in the general population, which, as every schoolboy knows, is "ten percent." This statistic is crucial for gay rights activists, for it shows that homosexual legal and political rights are a critical matter for a large portion of the population, and that a large number of individuals are suppressing their sexual nature for fear of the consequences. In the 1980's, the National Gay and Lesbian Task Force claimed to represent "23 million gay and lesbian persons," while some activists (and the mass media) often complained that the ten percent estimate was conservative. These, then, are the huge numbers of individuals supposedly subject to social and legal discrimination, who suffer when churches refuse to ordain gay clergy or perform same-sex marriages, or when the Armed Services exclude homosexuals. The suggestion of a huge "dark figure" of secret homosexuals is also convenient, as someone who opposes gay rights can be dismissed as being a closeted and self-hating homosexual.

There are countless problems with the "ten percent" theory, but two objections are decisive: one, that the research from which this figure is drawn is so flawed as to be worthless; and, two, that even the statistics that were produced should not be considered as evidence of a behavioral condition called "homosexual."

THE KINSEY STUDY

"One in ten" originated with the celebrated Alfred Kinsey study of the 1940's, which argued that about ten percent of men were chiefly or exclusively homosexual for at least three years between the ages of 16 and 55 (his claims for lesbianism rates among women were far lower). The original methodology, however, caused grave concern, not least over the ethical difficulties of reporting children's sexual responses in conditions which have been criticized for violating most accepted standards for the treatment of child research subjects. Indeed, the research has been denounced as formalized molestation in the disturbing but well-documented book *Kinsey, Sex and Fraud* by Judith Reisman and Edward Eichel. The study was also likely to produce a sizable overrepresentation of subjects who reported same-sex contacts both on a sporadic basis and as part of a continuing way of life. Kinsey and associates relied chiefly on volunteer subjects disproportionately drawn from metropolitan areas, and active homosexuals were overrepresented in the sample, as were college-educated individuals. In addition, a substantial number of subjects had institutional backgrounds, generally in jails or prisons. Later scholars were divided over whether the data might usefully be reinterpreted, or if the whole project is beyond salvage.

Already by the early 1970's, studies using methodologies superior to Kinsey's found the number of active homosexuals to be far less than popularly imagined. The size of the gay population became an urgent issue during these years because of the need to determine the population at special risk from AIDS, and in 1988, the estimated number of gay males in New York City alone was revised downward by some 80 percent. Several influential studies in the early 1990's revised the estimated homosexuality rate for men down even further, to between one and three percent. In 1993, the Alan Guttmacher Institute reported that between 1.8 and 2.8 percent of men surveyed reported at least one sexual contact with another man in the previous decade, while only about one percent had been exclusively homosexual in the previous year. This was in accord with the findings of a national survey recently undertaken in France. In 1994, a University of Chicago study found that 2.8 percent of men and 1.4 percent of women surveyed identified themselves as homosexual or bisexual. Though homosexual behavior varied by race and region, a figure approaching ten percent was recorded only for men living in the largest cities.

Putting these surveys together creates a convincing and surprising picture. Contrary to Kinsey's "one in ten," a figure of one in 30 would offer a more accurate assessment of the male population that can be described as homosexual or bisexual; and one in 60 would best represent the exclusively homosexual. The corresponding figures for women reporting sexual contacts with other women are somewhat lower. The cumulative evidence is now so overwhelming that any activist claiming that homosexuals represent "one man in ten" (still less one woman in ten) should ipso facto be discredited as an objective or credible authority. . . .

A "HIDDEN HOLOCAUST"?

In recent years, the impact of the "one in ten" mythology has been especially clear in the construction of a vast social problem, the general acceptance of which has made it easier to promote "gay rights" positions in education and other spheres. The epidemic in question is "gay teen suicide," meaning the statistics for suicide by young homosexuals. Suicide by teenagers and young adults has for some years been regarded as a grave social pathology, to which any parent of teenagers could imagine his or her child succumbing; but in the late 1980's, gay groups began to draw attention to the overrepresentation of young gay men and lesbians as victims of these tragic acts. As homosexuals were claimed to constitute at least a third of teen suicides, the panicked response to this issue should have been redirected to the threat to gay teens. To quote the gay newspaper The Advocate, "Gay and lesbian teenagers are killing themselves in staggering numbers. They are hanging themselves in high school classrooms, jumping from bridges, shooting themselves on church altars, cutting themselves with razor blades, and downing lethal numbers of pills. A conservatively estimated 1,500 young gay and lesbian lives are terminated every year because these troubled youths have nowhere to turn . . . because they cannot continue to live in a world that hates gays." It is a "hidden holocaust," a theme familiar from the AIDS controversy.

SKEWED STATISTICS

[Paul Gibson's claim that 30 percent of teen suicides are committed by gay youth] rested on Dr. Alfred Kinsey's discredited estimate that 10 percent of the population is gay. Moreover, his study included statistical impossibilities. For example, Gibson cites an author who stated in The Washington Blade (a homosexual newspaper) that as many as 3,000 gay youths commit suicide each year. However, since the total teen suicide rate stands at about 2,000 a year, Gibson's figures are not only highly exaggerated, but impossible.

Trudy Hutchens, Family Voice, August 1996.

Gay activists now use the teen suicide issue as one of their most effective rhetorical weapons, chiefly because of its appeal to audiences who might not normally be sympathetic. It is so attractive to the media because the theme easily lends itself to moving illustration in stories of young people who had killed themselves, the presumption being that homosexuality had been a determining factor in their decisions. The political consequences are far-reaching: if young gay lives are to be saved, then the schools and churches must reconsider their attitudes and priorities, eliminating antigay prejudices; "gay-positive" materials must be introduced into school curricula, and gay students "mainstreamed." In Massachusetts, especially, the urgency of the apparent crisis has led Republican Governor Bill Weld to establish a special commission on gay and lesbian youth, in order to recommend sweeping reforms throughout the state's educational system: after all, are not lives at stake? Gay teen suicide promises to be the trump card in local school board battles over the treatment of homosexuality in education.

The construction of the "epidemic" is a damning indictment of the use of social science in political debate, and the uncritical way in which tendentious statistics are accepted as fact. Briefly, gay teen suicide is an outright myth. Of course, some homosexual teenagers kill themselves, possibly in some cases as a result of insult, prejudice, or bullying, but there are no vaguely credible statistics about the scale of the issue.

MANUFACTURED STATISTICS

The manufacture of the "1,500 victims" is an example of *chutzpah*. In the late 1980's, the federal Department of Health and Human Services mounted an inquiry into the problem of teen suicide, defined as suicide by individuals aged 15 through 24. It commissioned dozens of papers, which were presented at various conferences around the country in 1986–87, and two of these studies involved sexual identity. One was a restrained and scholarly piece, which noted the scholarly consensus that homosexuals were two or three times more likely to kill themselves than heterosexuals, a well-substantiated finding. The other paper, however, was a polemical piece by San Francisco social worker Paul Gibson, and this is the *sole source* for current estimates of the numbers of gay teen suicides. This should be stressed: the figure derives not from an academic or a scholarly researcher, and the study was never subjected to any form of peer review. The author in question presented his views, which were then included without comment in the final report, and this was then cited in wildly misleading terms of "the federal government has conclusively shown that gay teen suicide is a vast epidemic." As [child psychiatrist] David Shaffer has remarked, the problem with "official statistics" is that they are often not official, and sometimes they are not even statistics.

So how did we get to the picturesque image of 1,500 people "hanging themselves in high school classrooms, jumping from bridges, shooting themselves on church altars" and so on? Though Gibson never explicitly states the basis for his argument, the logic appears to go as follows. First, some 5,000 young people commit suicide each year (true). Assuming that one-tenth of the population is homosexual, we would expect about 500 of these cases to involve gay teenagers and young adults, if homosexuals had a "normal" rate of suicidal behavior. However, homosexuals are approximately three times as likely as heterosexuals to commit suicide, so that the actual number of homosexual suicides in a given year would be closer to 1,500. Therefore, the proportion of teen and young adult suicide cases involving homosexuals is about 30 percent of the whole, or approximately one third.

The argument therefore depends on the estimate for the gay proportion of the population, and that is drawn entirely from Kinsey—neat and unadulterated by any of the subsequent refinements or revisions of that disastrous project, although many such interpretations were available even then. Gibson's conclusion has been quoted as authoritative by other writers, all of whom know (or should know) the fundamental flaws of the Kinsey data. Moreover, Gibson's "one in ten" refers to those young people with "a primary gay male, lesbian or bisexual orientation." What makes this outrageous is that not even Kinsey claimed a lesbianism rate of ten percent of women, even among the very odd sample with which he was working. Nor has any study ever shown or even argued that bisexuals have a higher tendency toward suicide than heterosexuals, as claims of higher suicide rates have only been presented for the exclusively and self-identified homosexual. Apples are most certainly being compared with oranges.

THE ABUSE OF SCIENCE

What is particularly strange about all this is that for most of this century, one of the standard weapons in the antihomosexual arsenal was the charge that gays were indeed likely to commit suicide because their condition was inherently unhealthy, and connected to various forms of mental illness. Countering this allegation, the American Psychiatric Association removed homosexuality from its diagnostic list of diseases and pathologies in 1973. A decade later, gay activists themselves began presenting gay vulnerability to suicide in the foreground of their own rhetoric, as proof of the pernicious effects of rampant and pervasive homophobia throughout American society. Today, this latter approach has become the norm, and the rhetoric has won universal acceptance in the media, for whom "homophobia" leads directly to the destruction of young lives.

The question of whether homosexuals (however defined) constitute one or ten percent of the population does not itself have great significance for the issue of gay rights or gay activism. One might follow [philosopher] John Stuart Mill in believing that a society has no business regulating the sexual doings of its citizens, provided that no harm is caused to outside parties, while there is ample precedent for providing legal protections for people or groups who prove vulnerable to assault or discrimination. These arguments do not change substantially whether the United States has two million "gays" or 25 million. On the other hand, it is hard to tolerate the arguments that have been made about gay rights and wrongs, when these are founded upon evidence or statistics that are not only wrong, but which the advocates in question should know are wrong. The whole mythology of "one in ten" of the population being homosexual might well be discussed in terms of abuse and perversion, but using neither term in a sexual sense: the abuse is that of rhetoric, and it is science which is perverted in the process.

| "Gay service members are now
allowed into the military, only to
face a series of tripwires intended to
flush them out."

THE "DON'T ASK, DON'T TELL"
POLICY IS A FAILURE

Andrew Sullivan

The Pentagon's "Don't Ask, Don't Tell" policy was established in
1993 as a means to prevent undue discrimination against gays
and lesbians in the military. The policy allows gay people to
serve in the military if they keep their sexual orientation confi-
dential; it also restricts the military's right to pursue information
about a service member's sexual orientation. In the following
viewpoint, Andrew Sullivan argues that the "Don't Ask, Don't
Tell" policy is a failure. The policy has been repeatedly violated,
he reports, and the harassment of gay military personnel is on
the increase. Such violations often result in discriminatory discharges of gay service members, Sullivan contends. Sullivan is a
senior editor of the weekly magazine *New Republic*. He is also the
author of *Virtually Normal: An Argument About Homosexuality*.

As you read, consider the following questions:
1. According to Sullivan, how many reported violations of the
   "Don't Ask, Don't Tell" policy occurred in 1997?
2. What is a "statement" case for discharging a gay service
   member from the military, according to the author?
3. In 1997, how many military commanders were disciplined
   for violating the "Don't Ask, Don't Tell" policy, according to
   Sullivan?

Reprinted from Andrew Sullivan, "Undone by 'Don't Ask, Don't Tell,'" *The New York Times*,
April 9, 1998, by permission. Copyright © 1998 by The New York Times.

" I think it's working," said Defense Secretary William Cohen, referring to the Pentagon's "don't ask, don't tell" policy for gay members of the armed services. He said this while announcing that discharges of homosexuals have increased by 67 percent since 1994. When you factor in the military's downsizing, the real figure is closer to 80 percent. If this is Mr. Cohen's definition of success, one wonders what failure would look like.

A GRIM PICTURE

The real picture is actually grimmer. Although "don't ask, don't tell" forbids military commanders from pursuing investigations of suspected homosexual conduct without compelling evidence, violations of the policy not to ask, pursue or harass homosexuals have soared, according to the Servicemembers Legal Defense Network, the only watchdog group tracking discharge cases under this policy.

The organization has documented 563 violations by military authorities of "don't ask, don't tell" in 1997, a jump from 443 violations in 1996. Reported cases of physical and verbal harassment of gay service members rose 38 percent from 1996 to 1997; cases in which military authorities illegally "asked" troops if they were gay increased 39 percent.

Until August of 1997, the military was still even using enlistment forms that directly asked about a person's sexual orientation. In its report, the Pentagon said the original form was preserved for four years "as a cost savings measure."

WITCH HUNTS

Witch hunts have continued. In 1996, an airman convicted of forcible sodomy at Hickam Air Force Base had a life sentence reduced to 20 months in return for outing 17 other allegedly gay servicemen. All the accused air force men were discharged; the rapist served less than a year.

Secretary Cohen's improbable defense is that the vast majority of discharges were voluntary. The proof? None in the Pentagon report, except for this: "The Services believe that most of the [cases involving a disclosure of homosexuality]—although not all of them—involve service members who voluntarily elected to disclose their sexual orientation to their peers, supervisors or commanders."

That's what it comes down to: "the Services believe . . ." The report later concedes that "because extensive inquiries or investigations are not conducted in most of these cases, the reasons for [the increase in numbers] are not known and would be difficult to ascertain." Compare this with the documentation of the Servicemembers Legal Defense Network.

The Pentagon further claimed that 80 percent of discharges were "statement" cases, implying that individuals were discharged after spontaneously declaring their orientation to their superiors. But that is misleading at best. All that a "statement" case means is that the grounds for discharge arose from what a service member allegedly said, and not what he or she did.

Reprinted by permission of Kirk Anderson.

Such "statements" can include private confessions to therapists, friends, peers or family members that were subsequently reported to military authorities.

I asked Michelle Benecke, co-director of the Servicemembers Legal Defense Network, how many of the 1,300 people her group has helped in the last four years have truly voluntarily disclosed their orientation. "None that I've come across," she said.

A DISCRIMINATORY POLICY

To its credit, the Pentagon does admit in its report that it has a problem. While insisting that the policy is "generally being implemented properly," the military concedes that it has not been vigilant enough in policing anti-gay harassment. As it now stands, someone attacked for being gay cannot report the abuse without risking discharge as a result.

The report also acknowledges that some women have been intimidated into not reporting sexual harassment, because they are sometimes accused of being lesbians if they reject male advances. More needs to be done to inform commanders of the regulations, the report adds.

These admissions would be more encouraging if the record was not so damning. In 1997, despite the 563 reported violations of "don't ask, don't tell," not a single military commander was disciplined for misconduct.

It's now clear that the policy has not simply failed. It is far worse than what went on before. Gay service members are now allowed into the military, only to face a series of tripwires intended to flush them out. They have become, in effect, the unintended bait of rogue military commanders. Other, more decent officers (and there are many) simply do not know the rules, since the Pentagon has done a poor job of telling them.

What to do about this? The Pentagon has embraced a mix of spin, denial and confession. The President has other options. In 1997, he denounced employment discrimination against homosexuals. But as Commander in Chief, Bill Clinton has now fired more homosexuals than any other employer in America. Is it too much to ask that this President finally live up to his own words? Or with this President, is that now utterly beside the point?

"[The 'Don't Ask, Don't Tell'] policy,
if honored, protects everyone in the
service, the straight no less than the
gay."

THE "DON'T ASK, DON'T TELL" POLICY COULD BE BENEFICIAL

Lars-Erik Nelson

The military's "Don't Ask, Don't Tell" policy, initiated by the Clinton administration in 1993, allows homosexuals to serve if they keep their sexual orientation private. Many commentators maintain that the policy has not curbed discrimination against gays in the military. In the following viewpoint, syndicated columnist Lars-Erik Nelson grants that the "Don't Ask, Don't Tell" policy has not stopped individuals from using charges of homosexuality to harass or expel military personnel. However, he contends, if the policy were properly executed, it would protect gays as well as heterosexuals falsely accused of being homosexual.

As you read, consider the following questions:
1. According to Nelson, what happened to Shannon Emery after she was attacked in a barracks?
2. In what way can false accusations of homosexuality be used as a form of sexual harassment, according to the author?
3. In the opinion of Michelle Benecke, cited by Nelson, why is the "Don't Ask, Don't Tell" policy a "double-whammy"?

Reprinted from Lars-Erik Nelson, "Straights, Gays, False Charges," *Liberal Opinion Week*, March 25, 1996, by permission of the Los Angeles Times Syndicate. Copyright ©1996 New York Daily News. Distributed by Los Angeles Times Syndicate.

D runken American soldiers attack a female military police officer in a barracks in South Korea. She yells, "Rape!" They whisper, "Lesbian."

Guess who winds up being court-martialed?

Pfc. Shannon Emery, the MP, finally beat this rap—but it took her 10 months of fighting before she was cleared and allowed to continue her career.

FALSE CHARGES OF HOMOSEXUALITY

It was too much to expect that President Bill Clinton's "Don't Ask, Don't Tell" policy, instituted in 1993, would resolve the difficult issues of homosexuality in the armed forces. But the Emery case makes it clear that "Don't Ask, Don't Tell" has not even halted the age-old military practice of using false charges of homosexuality to harass and expel perfectly straight heterosexuals.

"Women are particularly vulnerable to false claims (of lesbianism) as a means of sexual harassment," says a report issued by the Servicemembers Legal Defense Network. "For example, when a female service member rebuffs the sexual advances of men, reprimands a male subordinate for inferior performance or simply competes against men for a job opening, she often finds herself accused of 'lesbian conduct' in retaliation."

This sort of harassment is not unique to the military or to women. You perhaps know of the football star who was labeled "gay" because he preferred to study economics textbooks rather than chase cocktail waitresses. You may know of the awkward spinster who is dubbed a lesbian because she is big and gawky and has never married. I could tell you of an FBI agent, a gifted artist, who had to paint in secret lest J. Edgar Hoover (of all people!) find out about his "artiness" and brand him a homosexual.

The difference is that in today's military, false accusations of homosexuality still carry a potential penalty of discharge.

Under the "Don't Ask, Don't Tell" policy, the armed forces are not supposed to hunt down homosexuals or inquire into the sexual practices of servicemen and women. The official policy was most clearly stated by former Chairman of the Joint Chiefs of Staff Colin Powell: "We won't witch-hunt. We won't chase. We will not seek to learn orientation."

It has not worked out that way in practice. Servicemen and women are still vulnerable to denunciation and rumor. And at least some officers in the Naval Investigative Service still have the mind-set of the Keystone Kops: They tried to blame the disastrous 1989 explosion aboard the battleship Iowa on a fictitious homosexual love affair gone awry.

"We still have a double-whammy," says Michelle Benecke, a lawyer and former Army captain who co-wrote the report. "The men try to prove they're straight by making advances toward the women or even harassing them. Then the women have a choice: They can be either seen as very promiscuous or lesbians."

PROTECTION FOR EVERYONE IN THE SERVICE

What the report makes clear is that the "Don't Ask, Don't Tell" policy, if properly implemented, does not simply protect gays and lesbians in military service. It also protects the quiet sailor who would rather read his Bible than visit brothels on shore leave—and who then gets dubbed "faggot" by carousing shipmates. It protects the tough female officer who pulls a unit into shape or the adventurous 23-year-old like Shannon Emery from being denounced as dykes—then discharged from the service on the basis of pure spite.

President Clinton took a lot of heat for defending "gays in the military," but the reality is that his policy, if honored, protects everyone in the service, the straight no less than the gay.

PERIODICAL BIBLIOGRAPHY

The following articles have been selected to supplement the diverse views presented in this chapter. Addresses are provided for periodicals not indexed in the *Readers' Guide to Periodical Literature*, the *Alternative Press Index*, the *Social Sciences Index*, or the *Index to Legal Periodicals and Books*.

David Barsamian	"Equality and Respect," *Z Magazine*, September 1996.
Richard L. Berke	"Chasing the Polls on Gay Rights," *New York Times*, August 2, 1998.
Joan Biskupic	"Rejecting Distinctions Based on Prejudice," *Washington Post National Weekly Edition*, May 27–June 2, 1996. Available from PO Box 1150, 15th St. NW, Washington, DC 20071.
Donald A. Dripps	"A New Era for Gay Rights?" *Trial*, September 1996.
John Gallagher	"Are We Really Asking for Special Rights?" *Advocate*, April 14, 1998.
David Gelernter	"Gay Rights and Wrongs," *Wall Street Journal*, August 13, 1998.
Issues and Controversies On File	"Gays in the Military," March 6, 1998. Available from Facts On File News Services, 11 Penn Plaza, New York, NY 10001-2006.
Dirk Johnson	"Gay-Rights Movement Ventures Beyond Urban America," *New York Times*, January 21, 1996.
J. Jennings Moss	"Losing the War," *Advocate*, April 15, 1997.
Christopher Ott	"How to Talk to Homophobes (You May Be Related to One)," *In the Family*, July 1998. Available from PO Box 5387, Takoma Park, MD 20913.
Norman Podhoretz	"How the Gay-Rights Movement Won," *Commentary*, March 1997.
Gabriel Rotello	"Gay and Lesbian Rights," *Social Policy*, Spring 1998.
Anna Marie Smith	"Homoeconomics," *Z Magazine*, July/August 1998.
Urvashi Vaid	"Seeking Common Ground," *Ms.*, September/October 1997.

James D. Wilets   "The Human Rights of Sexual Minorities,"
                         Human Rights, Fall 1995. Available from the ABA
                         Press for the Section of Individual Rights and
                         Responsibilities of the American Bar
                         Association, 750 N. Lake Shore Dr., Chicago,
                         IL 60611.

CHAPTER 3

SHOULD SOCIETY ENCOURAGE INCREASED ACCEPTANCE OF HOMOSEXUALITY?

CHAPTER PREFACE

In August 1997, the Provincetown, Massachusetts, school board approved a "safe schools" policy that forbids discrimination based on race, religion, gender, disability, or sexual orientation. This decision was an extension of the city's plan to curb gay-bashing—an effort that had helped reduce hate crimes from twenty-one cases in 1991 to two cases in 1997, supporters maintain. The new "safe schools" policy, however, drew media attention after the *Washington Times* printed an article entitled "Provincetown Preschoolers to Learn ABC's of Being Gay." For months afterwards, the city found itself at the center of a debate over whether schools should encourage students to accept homosexuality.

"We're not teaching anyone to be gay," contends Keith Bergman, the Provincetown city manager. "We're trying to equip our young people and ourselves so we can combat bias against . . . sexual orientation." Supporters of "safe schools" programs insist that antidiscrimination measures are necessary because a growing number of teenagers are identifying as gay or lesbian at younger ages. These youths, many educators claim, are often the target of harassment and abuse at school and thus must deal with intense feelings of shame and social isolation that put them at increased risk of dropping out, abusing drugs, and committing suicide. The antibias policies adopted by thousands of public schools, as well as the gay-straight alliances and support groups sponsored by hundreds of high schools, are geared toward preventing such outcomes, advocates maintain. According to *Christian Science Monitor* staff writer Scott Baldauf, "such efforts are often necessary for gay students to receive an education and, in some cases, to merely survive."

Critics of "safe schools" policies, on the other hand, argue that many school-age children are simply too young to understand the controversies surrounding homosexuality. Moreover, these critics contend, programs that encourage youths to respect homosexuality may conflict with values that are taught in the home. Arne Owens, a spokesman for the Christian Coalition, grants that antigay bullying and abuse in schools are never justified. However, he maintains, "There should be no government sanction, promotion, or approval of homosexuality. . . . To bring it into the public schools gives it a certain legitimacy, and it's a behavior that most of our supporters view as wrong."

Whether schools should address gay and lesbian issues is one of the debates in the following chapter that examines society's attitude toward homosexuality.

| "We must let [children] know that if they turn out to be gay or lesbian, they will still have our love and respect."

SOCIETY SHOULD ENCOURAGE INCREASED ACCEPTANCE OF HOMOSEXUALITY

Rayford Kytle

Society should encourage positive attitudes toward homosexuality, argues Rayford Kytle in the following viewpoint. Widespread prejudice against gays and lesbians causes intense feelings of shame and self-hatred among young people who are struggling to come to terms with a homosexual orientation, Kytle maintains. He contends that gay youth often act out these feelings of shame by engaging in such self-destructive activities as substance abuse, unsafe sex, and even suicide. To prevent such outcomes, Kytle concludes, society must encourage an attitude of acceptance and respect for all people regardless of their sexual orientation. Kytle is deputy director of the news office of the U.S. Public Health Service.

As you read, consider the following questions:
1. When did Kytle become aware of his sexual orientation?
2. How many years did it take for the author to accept his homosexuality?
3. In the early years of his gay life, how did Kytle try to reassure himself of his self-worth?

Adapted from Rayford Kytle's speech to employees of the U.S. Public Health Service, December 1993.

I want to tell everybody who has young people in their lives—parents, aunts and uncles, neighbors or just members of the community—that some of these young people are gay, and some are struggling, alone, to come to terms with their sexual orientation. I want everybody to know that they can help to create a climate of tolerance, acceptance, love and support for these kids, so that they care enough about themselves, think highly enough of themselves, to want to stay healthy and live fulfilling, responsible lives.

I want to tell what it was like for me growing up, coming to terms with being gay, and how HIV entered and influenced my life. I think the difficulties I had in developing a positive self-concept are still problems for many young gay people. And I think it is these problems that cause many young gay men to behave in ways that put them at high risk for becoming infected with HIV, the virus that causes AIDS.

GROWING UP "DIFFERENT"

Ever since early childhood I knew there was something different about me, but it had never been clear to me how I was different.

About the age of 15, in 1962, when I was in 10th grade, I began to be aware that I was sexually attracted to other males. No one "recruited" me, no one abused me. These feelings came from deep inside me.

I come from a good family, went to good schools and lived in good neighborhoods. I was popular in school, made good grades and was active in the church. I wanted to become a Presbyterian minister.

In spite of all these advantages and connections, as I began to be aware of my sexual orientation, I was completely alone. I had no role models, no positive images of gay men, no social support as a gay male, no one to turn to. I couldn't tell my family—it was just too horrible, too unacceptable, unspeakable. I couldn't tell my friends—the worst thing you could possibly be was queer. I couldn't tell my teachers or my pastor. The only place I saw to turn to was medicine. I read in a church guidance counselor's office that homosexuality could be cured, like a disease.

I spent the next 12 years in and out of therapy, trying to erase, to hide this important part of myself from others and, most of all, from myself.

FEELINGS OF SHAME

The climate of prejudice and ignorance about gay people that I grew up in interfered with my life and slowed my development as a self-respecting, responsible, contributing member of society. It caused me to grow up doubting myself, feeling ashamed and frightened of my deepest feelings. How was I to find my calling in life—my career, work to give my heart and soul to, a direction for my life—how was I to find what really mattered to me when there was such a deep and significant part of me that I was trying to ignore, to deny, to hide, to kill?

Accepting my sexual orientation at the age of 27 was a great awakening, like being born—finally accepting my feelings, my self, turning a light on inside and no longer running away from what I saw there. It took many more years for me to overcome the self-hatred and self-doubt I had learned and to develop a healthy sense of who I was and what I wanted to do with my life.

During those early years of my gay life, sex was for me a means of validation, of endorsement. I needed frequent assurance that people liked me and valued me, because I had so little self-esteem, so little self-respect. It took me a long time to understand my insecurity, to overcome it and to establish a committed monogamous relationship based on mutual understanding, respect and affection.

But by that time, I had become infected with HIV.

GAY YOUTH NEED POSITIVE IMAGES

I hope that by talking and writing about my experience with HIV, I can help young gay people learn the things that took me

---

HOMOPHOBIA

We live in a society that is often prejudiced against gay, lesbian, and bisexual people. Gay people are subjected to discrimination, rejection, verbal assaults, and even physical violence. There are many negative stereotypes about gay people that fuel this homophobia. Because of these attitudes, many lesbian, gay, and bisexual people keep the truth of their sexual orientation hidden away—they stay in the closet, invisible. . . .

Since most people are heterosexual, our society tends to assume everyone is—unless someone lets it be known otherwise. Revealing your sexual orientation—or coming out—isn't easy, because you often face some negative responses. But it's also hard to stay in the closet and hide your true self. Bisexuals, lesbians, and gay men make many difficult compromises along the way to try to be both true to themselves and to survive well in a sometimes unfriendly world.

Ellen Bass and Kate Kaufman, *Free Your Mind*, 1996.

---

so long to learn; I want them to learn these things earlier than I did—in time to protect them from HIV. I don't want them to waste their time and energy hiding from themselves; I want them to come to terms with their lives earlier than I did, to develop a healthy sense of self-respect and a sense of responsibility to themselves and to the community. I want them to find work that they are passionate about, that they are able to respond to with all their resources.

Our youth need positive images—images of gay people who are in committed relationships, who are responsible members of the community, images that promote healthy and responsible choices by gay youth. The period when they are beginning to become aware of their sexual orientation is when they are most vulnerable, most in danger of falling prey to the climate of intolerance toward gay people, most in danger of becoming isolated, most in danger of developing low self-esteem, which leads to self-destructive behaviors—alcohol and drug abuse and suicide. And to unsafe sex, which puts them at risk for all sexually transmitted diseases and particularly HIV.

We need to tell all our young people, gay or not, that they should wait to have sex until they really know who they are and have a healthy sense of self-respect, to wait until they are ready to commit to someone they really know, care about and respect—someone who really knows them, respects and cares about them.

PROMOTING HEALTHY ATTITUDES TOWARD SEXUALITY

If you have created a negative attitude toward homosexuality as a parent, relative, friend, teacher, pastor or neighbor, it may be too late to change that by the time you find out that your child is gay or lesbian. By then you may have done that child great harm. We must let children know at an early age that their sexuality is a beautiful part of their lives and that it is to be valued and protected and respected. We must let them know that if they turn out to be gay or lesbian, they will still have our love and respect and we will still be there for them, and that we want them to feel a part of the family and the community. I think the way we do this is to let young people know by our behavior and our attitudes that there are gays and lesbians who are respectable members of the community. We have to show young people by our behavior toward gays and lesbians in general that whether a person is good or bad, responsible or irresponsible does not depend on his or her sexual orientation any more than it does on his or her race, religion or gender.

> "We must still ask whether
> [a predisposition toward
> homosexuality] should be acted on
> or whether it should be resisted."

SOCIETY SHOULD NOT ENCOURAGE INCREASED ACCEPTANCE OF HOMOSEXUALITY

The Ramsey Colloquium

The Ramsey Colloquium is a group of Christian and Jewish scholars sponsored by the Institute on Religion and Public Life. In the following viewpoint, the colloquium maintains that the gay and lesbian movement is largely a result of the sexual revolution, which advocated liberation from allegedly oppressive societal institutions. The institution of the traditional marriage and family, however, provides the most moral and effective way to raise children, channel sexual passion, and build communities, assert the authors; self-restraint and sexual chastity should therefore be championed. Moreover, the authors argue, homosexual behavior is contrary to God's will, so efforts to promote and legitimize homosexual lifestyles must be resisted.

As you read, consider the following questions:

1. According to the colloquium, in what way has the sexual revolution trivialized sexuality?
2. Why must society not remain indifferent to attacks on the heterosexual norm, in the authors' opinion?
3. According to the authors, when is some discrimination necessary?

Excerpted from "Morality and Homosexuality," by the Ramsey Colloquium, First Things, March 1994. Reprinted by permission of the Institute on Religion and Public Life.

Homosexual behavior is a phenomenon with a long history, to which there have been various cultural and moral responses. But today in our public life there is something new that demands our attention and deserves a careful moral response.

The new thing is a gay and lesbian movement that variously presents itself as an appeal for compassion, an extension of civil rights to minorities and a cultural revolution. This movement aggressively proposes radical changes in social behavior, religion, morality and law.

As committed Christians and Jews, we share the uneasiness of most Americans with the proposals advanced by the gay and lesbian movement, and we seek to articulate some of the reasons for the largely intuitive and pre-articulate anxiety of most Americans regarding homosexuality.

DEFINITION BY DESIRE

While the gay and lesbian movement is indeed a new thing, its way was prepared by the so-called sexual revolution. That revolution is motored by presuppositions that ought to be challenged. Perhaps the key presupposition is that human health and flourishing require that sexual desire, understood as a "need," be acted upon and satisfied. Any discipline of denial or restraint has been popularly depicted as unhealthy and dehumanizing.

We insist, however, that it is dehumanizing to define ourselves by our desires alone. Nor does it seem plausible to suggest that what millennia of human experience have taught us to regard as self-command should now be dismissed as mere repression.

At the same time that the place of sex has been grotesquely exaggerated by the sexual revolution, it has also been trivialized. The mysteries of human sexuality are commonly reduced to matters of recreation or taste, not unlike one's preferences in diet, dress or sport. This peculiar mix of the exaggerated and the trivialized makes it possible for the gay and lesbian movement to demand, simultaneously, a respect for what is claimed to be most constitutively true of homosexuals and tolerance for what is, after all, simply a difference in "lifestyle."

It is important to recognize the linkages among the component parts of the sexual revolution. Permissive abortion, widespread adultery, easy divorce, radical feminism, and the gay and lesbian movement have not by accident appeared at the same historical moment. They have in common a declared desire for liberation from constraint—especially constraint associated with an allegedly oppressive culture and religious tradition. They also have in common the presupposition that the body is little more than an instrument for the fulfillment of desire, and that the fulfillment of desire is the essence of the self. Finally, they all rest on a doctrine of the autonomous self. We believe it is a false doctrine that leads neither to individual flourishing nor to social well-being.

THE NEED FOR SEXUALLY CHASTE RELATIONSHIPS

Marriage and the family—husband, wife and children, joined by public recognition and legal bond—are the most effective institutions for the rearing of children, for the directing of sexual passion and for human flourishing in community. At the same time, it remains true that there are legitimate and honorable forms of love other than marriage. Indeed, one of the goods at stake in today's disputes is a long-honored tradition of friendship between men and men, women and women, women and men.

In the current climate, it becomes imperative to affirm the reality and beauty of sexually chaste relationships. We do not accept the notion that self-command is an unhealthy form of repression on the part of single people, whether their inclination is heterosexual or homosexual. Put differently, the choice is not limited to heterosexual marriage on the one hand and relationships involving extramarital or homogenital sex on the other.

We cannot settle the dispute about the roots—genetic or environmental—of homosexual orientation. Although some scientific evidence suggests a genetic predisposition, we must still ask whether such a predisposition should be acted on or whether it should be resisted.

In a fallen creation, many quite common attitudes and behaviors must be straightforwardly designated as sin. Although we are equal before God, we are not born equal in terms of our strengths and weaknesses, our tendencies and dispositions, our nature and nurture. We cannot utterly change the hand we have been dealt by inheritance and family circumstances, but we are responsible for how we play that hand.

Inclination and temptation are not sinful, although they surely result from humanity's fallen condition. Sin occurs in the joining of the will, freely and knowingly, to an act or way of life that is contrary to God's purpose. Religious communities in particular must lovingly support all the faithful in their struggle against temptation, while at the same time insisting, precisely for the sake of the faithful, on the sinfulness of the homogenital and extramarital heterosexual behavior to which some are drawn.

THE IMPORTANCE OF THE HETEROSEXUAL NORM

Since there are good reasons to support the heterosexual norm, since it has been developed with great difficulty, and since it can be maintained only if it is cared for and supported, we cannot be indifferent to attacks upon it. The social norms by which sexual behavior is inculcated and controlled are of urgent importance for families and for society as a whole.

Advocates of the gay and lesbian movement have the responsibility to set forth publicly their alternative proposals. This means more than calling for liberation from established standards. They must clarify for all of us how sexual mores are to be inculcated in the young, who are particularly vulnerable to seduction and solicitation. Public anxiety about homosexuality is pre-eminently a concern about the vulnerabilities of the young. This, we are persuaded, is a matter of legitimate and urgent public concern.

Reprinted by permission of Chuck Asay and Creators Syndicate.

Gay and lesbian advocates sometimes claim that they are asking for no more than an end to discrimination, drawing an analogy with the early civil-rights movement. The analogy is unconvincing and misleading. Differences of race are in accord with—not contrary to—our nature, and such differences do not provide justification for behavior that is otherwise unacceptable.

Certain discriminations are in fact necessary within society; it is not too much to say that civilization itself depends on the making of such distinctions (between, finally, right and wrong). In our public life, some discrimination is in order—when, for example, in education and programs involving young people the intent is to prevent predatory behavior that can take place under the guise of supporting young people in their anxieties about their "sexual identity."

SUPPORT FOR MARRIAGE

It is necessary to discriminate between relationships. Gay and lesbian "domestic partnerships," for example, should not be socially recognized as the moral equivalent of marriage. Marriage and the family are institutions necessary for our continued social well-being. In an individualistic society that tends to liberation from all constraint, they are fragile institutions in need of careful and continuing support.

To endure (tolerance), to pity (compassion), to embrace (affirmation): That is the sequence of change in attitude and judgment that has been advanced by the gay and lesbian movement with notable success. We expect that this success will encounter certain limits and that what is truly natural will reassert itself, but this may not happen before more damage is done to innumerable individuals and to our common life.

3

|"A positive attitude toward
homosexual marriage and
ordination of gay men and lesbians
. . . is not only consistent with
Scripture but mandated by it."

CHRISTIANS SHOULD ACCEPT HOMOSEXUALITY

Alice Ogden Bellis

Christians should accept homosexuality, argues Alice Ogden Bellis in the following viewpoint. She maintains that although the Bible says nothing positive about homosexuality, Scripture must be examined in light of its cultural and historical context. For example, Bellis points out, the antihomosexual laws of the Old Testament are part of an ancient code that included restrictive rules on food and clothing—rules that today's Christians are free to ignore. Moreover, the author asserts, Jesus' teachings emphasize the importance of love and compassion, and the acceptance of society's outcasts as God's people. Bellis concludes that an intelligent, informed interpretation of Scripture is supportive—not condemning—of gays and lesbians. Bellis teaches Old Testament language and literature at Howard University School of Divinity in Washington, D.C.

As you read, consider the following questions:

1. In Bellis's opinion, what is subversive about the Book of Ruth?
2. What does the author mean by her assertion that "God's word comes to us in an earthen vessel"?
3. What three principles of interpretation does Bellis suggest people use when reading the Bible?

Reprinted from Alice Ogden Bellis, "When God Makes a Way," *The Other Side*, March/April 1995, by permission of *The Other Side*.

For many years, I was convinced that because the Bible had nothing positive to say about homosexuality—and because its few comments on the subject all seemed to be negative—the Bible had to be regarded as condemning all forms of homosexual practice. I was not homophobic. I liked many of the gay men and lesbian women I knew. Yet, intellectually, I found it difficult to read negative as positive.

Oddly enough, what began to change my approach to this issue—and to Scripture in general—was my study of women's stories in the Hebrew Bible. I was particularly moved by the Book of Ruth.

The Subversive Story of Ruth

Ruth is a sweet little story, but it is also highly subversive. Many scholars have concluded that the book was written in the post-exilic period, a period of Israelite history characterized by narrow exclusivism. Given this context, since Ruth was a Moabite, and the Moabites were among Israel's most hated enemies, she is an odd hero. Ruth's story undercuts the exclusive attitudes of her time, particularly the negative feelings toward foreign women, which we find expressed in Scripture in both Ezra and Nehemiah (Ezra 9:12; 10:1–44; Neh. 13:23–30).

Even more surprising is the fact that Ruth seems to overturn a biblical law which prohibits any Moabite from being part of the Israelite community for ten generations (Deut. 23:3). According to the genealogy at the end of Ruth (4:17), Ruth is the great grandmother of David. By this genealogy, David comes only three generations after Ruth. According to the law expressed in Deuteronomy, David was not legally a member of the Jewish community!

Of course, many scholars believe the Book of Ruth is a historical novelette, and that the genealogy at the end is an example of "creative" genealogy. Yet, whether historically accurate or not, its function is the same: to uphold God's inclusive love for all people—even foreign women, even Moabites. (This idea is explored further by André LaCocque in *The Feminine Unconventional: Four Subversive Figures in Israel's Tradition*.)

Realizing that the Book of Ruth contradicts the law of Deuteronomy has changed the way I view Scripture. The Bible is not static but dynamic. It must continually be reinterpreted by the religious community to fit each new historical context—sometimes even to the point of doing a 180-degree turn.

Over the centuries, advances in various fields of knowledge have occasionally caused the Christian community to reevaluate its methods of interpreting the Bible. The discovery that the earth is not flat but spherical, and that it revolves around the sun, not vice versa, forced interpreters to grapple with the biblical image of a flat earth at the center of the universe. This and other scientific findings have led most interpreters to conclude that the Bible is authoritative in matters of faith and morals but not in matters of science.

More recently, women's changing roles have pushed interpreters to develop hermeneutical principles for understanding the negative material in the Bible regarding women. For example, it seems clear that statements such as 1 Timothy 2:9, which claims that braided female hair is immodest, need to be regarded as human, culturally bound pronouncements. Many scholars have concluded that passages which seem to offer specific advice to specific people, such as the admonition for women to remain silent in church (1 Cor. 14:34), must be read in light of timeless statements such as, "There is no longer Jew or Greek, there is no longer slave or free, there is no longer male and female; for all of you are one in Christ Jesus" (Gal. 3:28).

We have been forced to realize that the treasure of God's Word comes to us in an earthen vessel, that is, a document containing many human features. The struggle to discern God's eternal Word in the midst of the human words of the Bible is not easy. But once we admit the human element in the Scriptures, we have no choice but to seek to hear God's voice through the human voices, rather than assuming the two are identical.

CHANGING ATTITUDES

Just as changing attitudes toward women's roles have fostered new principles of biblical interpretation, new information and attitudes regarding homosexuality are nudging biblical interpreters to reconsider their existing hermeneutical principles and, in some cases, to form new principles. I would like to suggest three governing principles of interpretation that can guide us as we explore scriptural teachings regarding homosexuality.

The first principle is that *biblical teaching must be viewed in light of its cultural context.* For example, when we read the biblical injunction to "be fruitful and multiply" (Gen. 1:28), we must keep in mind that at the time of this utterance, the Israelites needed to expand their population in order to survive and thrive. In today's world, where so many are in need, simply filling the world with more and more bodies is a recipe for destruction rather than survival.

Similarly, as Robin Scroggs noted in his landmark 1983 book

The New Testament and Homosexuality, the kinds of homosexual relationships prevalent in New Testament times were pederastic and exploitative. Biblical material condemning such practices (Rom. 1:26–27; 1 Cor. 6:9; 1 Tim. 1:10) should not be read as denunciation of the kind of monogamous homosexual bonds that exist today, but which were apparently extremely rare in Hellenistic times.

It is more difficult to determine the cultural background of the anti-homosexual laws in the Levitical code (Lev. 18:22; 20:13). But we should keep in mind that these passages are included in a body of law that promotes kosher food laws (Lev. 11; 20:25), prohibits sexual intercourse with a menstruating woman (Lev. 18:19), and forbids wearing clothing made of a mixture of fibers (Lev. 19:19). Christians usually feel free to ignore these laws, following Paul who taught that Christians were not required to follow Jewish requirements such as circumcision (1 Cor. 7:19; Gal. 5:6; 6:15; Eph. 2:15).

The Sodom and Gomorrah story in Genesis 19 is not really about homosexuality but rather about homosexual rape. Like all rape, it is more a matter of power than sex. In this story and the similar passage in Judges 19, the point was to humiliate threatening outsiders by treating them like women. The misogynist ideology behind the practice should be noted.

INFORMED BIBLICAL READING

The second hermeneutical principle I would stress is this: *Biblical teaching should be read in light of later teaching on the same subject, the general direction of Scripture, and, for Christians, especially Jesus' teaching.*

It is not widely known that within the Hebrew Bible, earlier laws are sometimes challenged by later teaching. For example, as Walter Brueggemann has pointed out in *Using God's Resources Wisely: Isaiah and Urban Possibility*, Isaiah 56:3 criticizes Deuteronomy 23:1, which declares that no eunuchs shall ever be part of the Israelite religious community. It is not enough to understand Deuteronomy 23:1 in its cultural context alone; we must also be aware of what Isaiah said on the matter. Since Isaiah came after Deuteronomy and both are in the canon, the teaching of Isaiah on this matter takes precedence over that in Deuteronomy.

In a similar way, Jesus reinterpreted laws governing marriage and divorce, as well as adultery. Jesus responded to these laws not with a new legalism but with an understanding of the purpose of marriage (Matt. 5:27–28, 31–32; 19:3–9; Mark 10:11–12; Luke 16:18; John 8:3–11).

Unfortunately, we have no record of Jesus saying anything

specifically about homosexuality. Yet Jesus did give us moral principles to guide us in all ethical matters. When asked about the most important law, he replied that the greatest law is that we should love God with all of our heart, soul, mind, and strength. This is the Shema from Deuteronomy 6:4, quoted in Matthew 22:37, Mark 12:29–30, and Luke 10:27. The second law Jesus gave is that we should love our neighbors as ourselves (Lev. 19:18, quoted in Matt. 22:39). It's difficult to derive a negative understanding of homosexuality from these laws.

Another View

Signe Wilkinson/Cartoonists & Writers Syndicate. Reprinted with permission.

Moreover, Jesus continued the direction established in several books of the Hebrew Bible by including those who were considered outcasts as part of God's people. The Old Testament Book of Ruth included the hated Moabites. Jonah extended God's love to the Ninevites. Jesus included the Samaritans (John 4:7–30), tax collectors (Luke 19:1–10), and "bad" women (Luke 7:36–39).

If Jesus were alive today, and a person were "caught" in a homosexual act and brought before him, what would he do? Would he tell the homosexual to "go and sin no more" (John 8:11), or would he turn the tables on the accusers by telling the story of "the good homosexual" (Samaritan) (Luke 10:29–37)? Perhaps, if the sexual act were exploitative or casual, Jesus might have told the first story, since he regarded the sexual union of two persons as a sacred trust not to be violated. But since there are many monogamous gay unions, it is equally possible that he would have told the second story.

THE SPIRIT OF BIBLICAL LAW

The third hermeneutical principle is that the Bible should not be read as a blueprint for living so much as an architectural school where we find the tools we need to build our lives. As in schools, certain basics will never change, but other aspects of the curriculum are endlessly reworked.

The biblical authors employed far greater freedom in interpreting their traditions than is generally recognized. When Matthew used Isaiah 7:14 as the basis for his Immanuel prophecy (Matt. 1:22–23), he totally reinterpreted the text. It was not originally a messianic prophecy but a prophecy of deliverance from an immediate historical crisis. A young woman, already pregnant, would survive the crisis and bear the child. This was the sign of God's presence with the community.

Similarly, Jesus reinterpreted much Hebrew law, explaining that he came to fulfill it, that is, to bring it to its proper conclusion, not to throw it out (Matt. 5:17–18; Mark 13:31; Luke 16:17). He was criticized for his unorthodox behavior (Matt. 12:1–8; Mark 2:15–17,23–36; Luke 5:29–32; 6:1–5; 7:39). He in turn criticized the establishment for living by the letter of the law rather than by its spirit (Matt. 23:23–24; Luke 11:42).

Jesus' creative approach can be seen in his response to the disciples' request that he teach them how to pray. Jesus did not teach them by rote. In spite of the long tradition of repeating the Lord's Prayer verbatim each Sunday, Jesus did not say to pray by repeating his exact words, at least according to the text in Matthew. Rather he told his disciples to pray "like this"—he gave them a model, an idea to emulate.

We may wonder if all this gives us the right to be as creative with the tradition as Jesus was. We may fear that this opens up a world of subjectivity. Does such an approach mean we must consider all interpretations to be equally valid? Somewhere I read of a woman who interpreted Paul's admonition to "put on the new man" (Eph. 4:24) as a mandate for her to get a new husband. It seems that such "creative" approaches are clearly against the grain of the Spirit of the Bible. How can we know if our interpretations are right?

The short answer is we can't. There is no guarantee that any of us will interpret the Scriptures accurately. But there are some important indicators. As we evaluate and reevaluate our own understandings, we must pay careful attention to important clues such as the inner witness of the Holy Spirit, the consistency of our interpretation with the overall thrust of Scripture, and, in the long run, the acceptance of the Christian community.

It is true that the Bible never says anything positive about homosexuality. In spite of this, and after years of considering the matter, I have made a 180-degree turn in my understanding of the Bible on this issue. I have concluded that a positive attitude toward homosexual marriage and ordination of gay men and lesbians for the Christian ministry is not only consistent with Scripture but *mandated* by it.

Moreover, I feel that God has again made a way where there appeared to be no way. I marvel at the richness of the Scriptures, the subtlety of God, and the joy of new perspectives.

"Today the 'gay lifestyle' has grabbed
a lot of attention, and many people
twist the Scriptures to justify the
sin."

CHRISTIANS SHOULD NOT ACCEPT HOMOSEXUALITY

D. James Kennedy

Christians must continue to recognize that homosexuality is a
sin, contends D. James Kennedy in the following viewpoint. Despite homosexual activists' arguments to the contrary, the Bible
clearly teaches that homosexual behavior is unnatural and
wrong, Kennedy maintains. However, he points out, the Christian position on homosexuality does not condone the hatred of
people who engage in homosexual activity. Christians should, in
fact, denounce homosexuality while supporting the efforts of
people to stop committing homosexual sin, he argues. Kennedy
is senior minister of Coral Ridge Presbyterian Church in Fort
Lauderdale, Florida. He is also chancellor of Knox Theological
Seminary in Fort Lauderdale.

As you read, consider the following questions:

1. According to Kennedy, why was the city of Sodom destroyed?
2. Why must Christians avoid hatred, according to the author?
3. What is the difference between "defining deviancy down"
   and "defining deviancy up," according to Kennedy?

Reprinted from D. James Kennedy, "Leading Voices Under Attack," Moody, March/April
1996, with permission.

R ecently, a leader in the homosexual rights movement asked to see me. Toward the end of our meeting he said one of the most astonishing things I've ever heard on the subject. "The Bible nowhere even mentions homosexuality," he stated.

Unfortunately, our time was over and I couldn't discuss with him what the Scriptures do say. Today the "gay lifestyle" has grabbed a lot of attention, and many people twist the Scriptures to justify the sin.

God's Word, however, is clear:

"If a man lies with a man as one lies with a woman, both of them have done what is detestable" (Lev. 20:13).

"God gave them over to shameful lusts. Even their women exchanged natural relations for unnatural ones. In the same way the men also abandoned natural relations with women and were inflamed with lust for one another" (Rom. 1:26, 27).

"Do not be deceived: Neither the sexually immoral nor idolaters nor adulterers nor male prostitutes nor homosexual offenders, nor thieves nor the greedy nor drunkards nor slanderers nor swindlers will inherit the kingdom of God" (1 Cor. 6:9,10).

"That is what some of you were," Paul added. "But you were washed, you were sanctified, you were justified in the name of the Lord Jesus Christ and by the Spirit of our God" (v. 11).

A VISIT TO SODOM

One of the most familiar passages about homosexuality is in Genesis 19. The Lord and two angels, appearing as men, came to the city of Sodom at evening. Lot graciously invited them to spend the night in his home. But before they went to sleep, the men of the city surrounded the house. "Where are the men who came to you tonight?" they demanded. "Bring them out to us so that we can have sex with them" (v. 5).

Such flagrant wickedness is the reason the Lord destroyed the city (vv. 12, 13). Yet some today claim that this story has no relevance to the modern issue of homosexuality. The sin of Sodom was inhospitality, they say, or pride or disregard for the poor.

The people of Sodom were clearly inhospitable. They were proud, wealthy, and had no concern for the poor (Ezek. 16:49). But they also committed sexual abominations. It was this sin that caused their destruction.

A brochure from a pro-homosexual church asks, "Why do all the other passages of Scripture referring to this account [Sodom] fail to raise the issue of homosexuality?" That question ignores the words of Jude:

"In a similar way, Sodom and Gomorrah and the surrounding

towns gave themselves up to sexual immorality and perversion. They serve as an example of those who suffer the punishment of eternal fire" (v. 7).

The message could not be clearer. If the Bible does not teach that sodomy is a sin, it doesn't teach anything is a sin.

HATING SIN, LOVING SINNERS

How do people respond today when we say that homosexual behavior is a sin? They say we are homophobes, that we are filled with hate.

Someone has said that this accusation is like calling the Surgeon General a smokophobe. When he put the health warning on cigarette packages, did that prove he hated smokers? Most smokers probably have family members who have tried to dissuade them from smoking. Is that because of hate? No! It's because of love.

A study of First John makes it clear that we must not hate. "Anyone who claims to be in the light but hates his brother is still in the darkness" (2:9). "Dear children, let us not love with words or tongue but with actions and in truth" (3:18). "Whoever does not love does not know God, because God is love" (4:8).

The Christian position is that we must love the sinner but hate the sin. I think robbery is a terrible sin, and I hate it. I think rape is a terrible sin, and I hate it. I think the same about murder and many other sins. But that doesn't mean I hate the people who do them. I have counseled with them and prayed for them and witnessed to them.

Likewise, I have counseled with some who have committed homosexual sin. I know some who have come out of that lifestyle. I know some who are still struggling to overcome it. And I know others who want to stay there. As followers of Christ, our prayer must be that all will be set free.

WHAT ARE THE FACTS?

Tragically, some today insist that people can't be set free from homosexuality. They say it is something they are born with, that there is nothing they can do about it.

The Kinsey Report claimed that 10 percent of American men were homosexuals. More reliable studies of recent years have put the total closer to 1 or 2 percent. One study showed that 2 percent of American men admitted some homosexual activity in the past, but not in the present. This suggests that there may be more ex-homosexuals in America than active homosexuals. So much for the lie that people can't change!

What about recent studies indicating that homosexuality may be genetic? Each of those studies has serious scientific flaws. But even if the studies suggest predisposing factors, they do not prove determinative factors. People have different kinds of personalities. Some are aggressive, others shy. Some have tendencies toward alcoholism or hot-headedness. That does not mean society should put its imprimatur on those things as being right.

REDEFINING DEVIANCY

Christians in America need to understand the goals of the homosexual activists. Now that homosexuals have gotten themselves into positions of influence, they are trying to move society in their direction.

The process involves two parts: *D.D. Down* and *D.D. Up*. The first means "defining deviancy down." When deviancy becomes prevalent in a society, people tend to make the definition of deviancy smaller. Otherwise, it is too uncomfortable to deal with. An example of this occurred several years ago when the American Psychiatric Society declared that homosexuality was no longer a pathological condition.

A DEFORMATION OF THE CREATED ORDER

Naturally I accept the authority of Scripture in condemning homosexual conduct, but the Bible's condemnation does not in itself make it wrong; rather Scripture condemns it because it *is* wrong. God does not make it wrong by an arbitrary act of will; it is wrong because it is a deformation of that created order which God declared in Genesis to be good. Quite obviously God created man as male and female; not merely the biblical text but the very structure of our bodies shows that male and female are made for each other. And the *bodies* of homosexuals are no different in this respect. They too proclaim the truth of Genesis, that the male and the female are for each other.

Thomas Storck, *New Oxford Review*, May 1997.

D.D. Up is the opposite. It means taking what has always been known as normal and defining that up into deviancy. As one writer explains, "That distracts us from real deviancy and gives us the feeling that, despite the murder and mayhem and madness around us, we are really preserving and policing our norms."

Do you know who the new social deviates are? Anyone who says that homosexuality is wrong or sinful. That's why homosexual rights activists march in front of churches with signs saying, "Stop the Hate." (They don't mention the threats or vandalism committed by some radical homosexuals.)

Churches are not the only target. Today there are psychologists and psychiatrists who seek to restore homosexuals to a heterosexual lifestyle. Attempts are being made to have such therapists declared unethical. They are abusing psychiatry, the activists say.

The homosexual agenda may be most dangerous in the public schools. One study suggests that 26 percent of 12-year-old boys have sexual ambiguities. By age 17, that drops to 5 percent, and by age 21 probably to about 2 percent. But in some schools young children are hearing that "Heather has two mommies" and "Johnny has two daddies"—and that it's perfectly normal. Talk about creating sexual confusion!

TAKING OUR STAND

When Lot resisted the demands of the men of Sodom, they accused him of being judgmental. "This fellow came here as an alien, and now he wants to play the judge!" (Gen. 19:9). We will probably hear similar accusations.

In addition, homosexual activists will work hard at convincing us that they are the victims in this controversy. The book *After the Ball* explains their strategy: "In any campaign to win over the public, gays must be portrayed as victims in need of protection so that straights will not be inclined to refuse to adopt the role of protector. . . . We must forego the temptation to strut our gay pride publicly to such an extent that we undermine our victim image."

We must not let the ploys and accusations of the homosexual movement keep us from our responsibility to speak the truth in love. America is being conned, and the consequences are serious. May God give us the wisdom to wake up while we have time.

"Schools must take specific steps to make hallways, classrooms, and playing fields safe and accommodating [for gay youth]."

SCHOOLS SHOULD STRESS ACCEPTANCE OF HOMOSEXUALITY

Shelly Reese

In the following viewpoint, Shelly Reese argues that educators must take action to curb the prevalence of homophobia and gay-bashing in schools. Schools should adopt educational programs and services that emphasize respect for gays and lesbians, the author contends. Adding sexual orientation to antidiscrimination policies, providing gay adult role models, initiating student support groups, and including library information on gay and lesbian issues are healthy ways to address the topic of homosexuality in schools, asserts Reese. Reese is a freelance writer based in Cincinnati, Ohio.

As you read, consider the following questions:

1. According to Reese, how many gay and lesbian adolescents are there in the United States?
2. According to Norma Bailey, cited by the author, how many gay and lesbian students drop out of school?
3. What kind of "silent symbols" could schools provide to help gay youths feel less isolated, according to Reese?

Reprinted from Shelly Reese, "The Law and Gay-Bashing in Schools," *High Strides*, March/April 1997, with permission from National Middle School Association.

Most people would consider it a tragedy that a middle-school student suffered beatings, verbal harassment, and a mock rape because of his sexual orientation. In November 1996, a federal court in Eau Claire, Wisconsin, put it in even stronger terms, calling it a crime.

A Wisconsin jury awarded almost $1 million to Jamie Nabozny and agreed that a middle-school principal and two high-school administrators at Nabozny's former schools in Ashland, Wisconsin, had violated his civil rights by failing to intervene and stop the abuse after he went to them for help.

Nabozny, now 21, was a seventh-grade honor student at Ashland Middle School when he began reporting fellow students for throwing metal bolts and pencils at him on the school bus, slapping him, pulling his chair out from under him, and pretending to rape him.

Despite complaints by Nabozny and his parents, the abuse continued and intensified. By high school, Nabozny's classmates had beaten him and urinated on him. The abuse became so unbearable that Nabozny, who never denied he was gay, attempted suicide three times and ultimately dropped out of high school when he was in the eleventh grade.

When the time came for the law suit to be tried in court, Nabozny was represented by the Lambda Legal Defense and Education Fund. That organization now has available a manual it has prepared, *Stopping Anti-Gay Abuse of Students in Public Schools: A Legal Perspective*, which is geared toward teachers, parents, and students and includes an appendix of resources.

THE PLIGHT OF GAY YOUTH

The case has cast a national spotlight on the plight of gay and lesbian youths and could have repercussions for schools nationwide. Although there are an estimated 2.9 million gay and lesbian adolescents in the United States, many schools—uncomfortable with the issue or unaware of the extent of the abuse—have been slow to include sexual orientation in their anti-discrimination policies.

For homosexual students, that omission has transformed schools from institutions of learning to places where verbal harassment, beatings, and even rape are all too common.

"This is an issue of bottom-line safety for students, end of story," says Rea Carey, who is the director of the National Youth Advocacy Coalition. "For many gay and lesbian students, from the moment they walk in the school's doors to the moment they leave, they are harassed and verbally and physically abused. It's hard to learn and accomplish the developmental tasks of adolescence in that environment."

The National Youth Advocacy Coalition, which provides support to gay and lesbian youth, was recently joined by The Bridges Project of the American Friends Service Committee, which facilitates communication among gay-youth service-providers. . . .

SOCIAL OSTRACISM

Because of the hostile environment, an estimated 28 percent of gay and lesbian students drop out of school, according to Norma Bailey, an assistant professor of middle-level education at Central Michigan University and a frequent public speaker on the topic.

Other homosexual students face even greater dangers. The isolation and hostility gay and lesbian adolescents encounter make them two to three times more likely to commit suicide than heterosexual youths, according to a 1989 report by the U.S. Department of Health and Human Services. That report also indicates that, similarly, low self-esteem and social alienation make gay and lesbian youths three times more likely to abuse drugs and alcohol.

Homosexual youths also are at risk of contracting sexually transmitted diseases because a high percentage of them experiment sexually. Lesbian girls, in an attempt to hide their sexual orientation, are far more likely than their heterosexual peers to become pregnant.

The social ostracism which homosexuals experience often catches heterosexual youths in its cruel net. A survey which was released in the fall of 1996 by the Safe Schools Coalition, in Washington state, found that for every gay, lesbian, or bisexual youth who reported being harassed at school, four heterosexual youths were targeted for abuse because they were perceived to be homosexual.

The Coalition, which has been documenting cases of homosexual abuse for three years, found that 34 percent of gay, lesbian, and bisexual students and 8 percent of all students had suffered antigay harassment at school because "somebody hung a label on them," according to Arlis Stewart, a spokeswoman for the Coalition and also director of the American Friends Service Committee.

Despite these documented dangers, middle schools have hesitated to address the issue of homosexual discrimination. Bailey attributes it to a lack of understanding. In a survey of Colorado teachers, she found that about 65 percent had never taken a course at the undergraduate or graduate level that included information about homosexuality, and about 82 percent had never participated in a professional development session on the topic.

"Homophobia in our country is not so much bigotry as ignorance, and ignorance can only be conquered through education," she said.

Youth advocates say that while the educational programs that exist tend to be geared toward high-school students and educators, they might be more important for middle-school students, many of whom are confused about issues of sexuality.

CREATING SAFER ENVIRONMENTS

To help students—both homosexual and heterosexual—learn respect for themselves and others, schools must take specific steps to make hallways, classrooms, and playing fields safe and accommodating, says Kevin Jennings, of the Gay, Lesbian, and Straight Teachers Network (GLSTN), a national organization that brings together gay and straight teachers to combat homophobia in schools and to support gay teachers.

GAY AND LESBIAN ROLE MODELS

Studies consistently show that personal acquaintance with gay and lesbian people is the most effective means for developing positive attitudes toward acceptance. Both gay and straight students benefit from having role models such as openly gay and lesbian teachers, coaches, and administrators. Straight students are offered an alternative to the stereotypes with which they have often been raised. Gay and lesbian students get the chance, often for the first time, to see healthy gay and lesbian adults, which gives them hope for their own future.

Schools need to create the conditions necessary for gay and lesbian faculty to feel safe in "coming out." If no role models are available from within the school community, the school can bring in presenters from a local gay and lesbian speakers bureau or from a college gay and lesbian student association.

Norma J. Bailey and Tracy Phariss, *Education Digest*, October 1996.

Jennings' suggestions include that schools:

• Guarantee equality by adding "sexual orientation" to their nondiscrimination statements and publicizing their policies of equal treatment for all students.

• Create a safe environment by developing procedures for

handling cases of harassment and establishing consequences for offenders.

• Provide adult role models by allowing gay faculty members to "come out" so they can help dispel inaccurate stereotypes about homosexuals. If no role models are available on campus, schools can invite local gay and lesbian associations to speak to students.

• Provide support for students. Peer support and acceptance are critical to adolescents. "Gay-Straight Alliances" can help students understand issues which involve homophobia and sexual orientation regardless of their own sexual orientation.

• Diversify library holdings to include materials on gay and lesbian issues and reassess the school's curriculum. Teachers might address the impact of sexual identity on literature by gay and lesbian writers, such as Virginia Woolf and Walt Whitman.

Schools also can provide students with "silent symbols," Stewart says. Posters with telephone help lines or a "safe person"—a designated counselor or teacher—can help youths feel less isolated and hopeless, she notes.

PROVIDING INFORMATION

"If you can't deal with the issue as an adult, at least direct kids to the information," says Irvin Howard, an education professor at California State University at San Bernardino and a member of the board of directors for the California League of Middle Schools. "You don't have to agree or disagree, you just have to be able to refer them to someplace where they can find help."

One program that is showing promising results in the Seattle area involves bringing gay and lesbian youth into middle- and high-school classrooms to talk about their own experiences. During the past five years, for example, 20-year-old Naomi (who asked that her last name not be used for fear of harassment) has visited about 100 middle-school classrooms in the Seattle area as part of the Safe Schools program, a statewide partnership of agencies and civic organizations that works to make schools safer for homosexual students and educators.

Naomi, who tried to kill herself at age 12 and ran away from home at age 13, said she is painfully aware of the pressures that gay and lesbian students encounter in school. In high school, for example, Naomi's male classmates threatened to "rape her and straighten her out." They also beat up her best friend on campus because he is gay.

Although she hopes that her school presentations will make students feel less alone, Naomi also wants to help dispel some popular misconceptions about homosexuality. She considers it progress when middle-school students ask enlightened questions, such as whether she ever wants to have a family and settle down with one woman and have babies. "That's exciting to me," she said, "because it's important that they know I do want these things, and I live a pretty normal life."

VIEWPOINT

"The sight of teachers standing before
the entire school body in support of
homosexuality has a coercive
influence upon children that is
frightening."

SCHOOLS SHOULD NOT STRESS
ACCEPTANCE OF HOMOSEXUALITY

Ed Vitagliano

Schools should not advocate respect for homosexuality, argues
Ed Vitagliano in the following viewpoint. He maintains that pro-
homosexual school programs undermine the authority and the
moral values of parents who believe that homosexuality is
wrong. In Vitagliano's opinion, such programs manipulate children by presenting the pro-gay position as the only "correct"
stance on homosexuality. These school programs also wrongly
imply that the traditional Christian opinion on homosexuality is
a form of bigotry, the author contends. Vitagliano is news editor
of the *American Family Association Journal*, a monthly periodical that
focuses on the media's influence on the American family.

As you read, consider the following questions:

1. According to Vitagliano, which groups funded the video *It's
   Elementary*?
2. In what specific ways do teachers subtly coerce students into
   supporting homosexuality, according to the author?
3. How did the eighth-grade teacher Kim Coates change her
   students' minds about homosexuality, according to
   Vitagliano?

Abridged from Ed Vitagliano, "Pro-Homosexual Video Targets Public Schools," *AFA Journal*,
June 1997. Reprinted by permission.

The battle in this country between those holding to traditional morality and those espousing hedonism has reached a fever pitch, manifested in no clearer terms than the ideological conflict over homosexuality. But forget about same-sex marriage, employment discrimination or AIDS funding. There may be no area of debate that causes blood pressures to escalate more rapidly than the question of whether public schools should teach children about homosexuality.

Now the homosexual community has thrown down the gauntlet by unveiling a video entitled *It's Elementary: Talking About Gay Issues in School*, and as its title implies, the video is aimed at the educational establishment. The video is produced by Helen Cohen and Debra Chasnoff, the latter an Academy Award–winning documentary producer. In 1992 Chasnoff became the first woman to openly declare her lesbianism at the Oscars.

The producers went into six elementary and middle schools where teachers and principals are already force-feeding children with pro-gay grist. The narrator says the educators allowed the filming "in the hope of inspiring other educators and parents to take the next step in their own school communities to teach children respect for all."

TEACHING ABOUT THE "GAY LIFESTYLE"

The video was funded largely by the San Francisco–based Columbia Foundation, as well as People for the American Way, the Gay & Lesbian Alliance Against Defamation, and the California Teacher Association's Gay and Lesbian Caucus. The film also credits the National Endowment for the Arts (NEA) with a hand in helping to fund the project.

It's Elementary has picked up several awards, including the prestigious C.I.N.E. Golden Eagle for the Best Teacher Education Film of 1996. Targeted to state departments of education and local school boards, the video has been screened in at least six states, and California Assemblywoman Sheila J. Kuehl, an open lesbian, said she intends to have it shown in all 50 states.

The narrator's voice calmly introduces the video while the camera pans over a playground full of children playing peacefully together at a public school. "Most adults probably don't see why schools should teach young children about gay people," the voice says. While that is no doubt true, it becomes clear in *It's Elementary* that homosexual activists see why schools should teach about the gay lifestyle.

It is to capture the hearts and minds of the next generation. In fact, in an interview about the video with a Santa Fe newspaper, Chasnoff states candidly, "What's clear in the film is that the younger the kids, the more open they were. . . . If we could start doing this kind of education in kindergarten, first grade, second grade, we'd have a better generation."

OUT OF THE MOUTHS OF BABES

"Most adults probably don't see . . ." becomes the theme of this documentary, portraying the ignorance and bigotry of adults—including parents—as the fountainhead of homophobia. In contrast, pro-homosexual statements are heard coming from the mouths of children, shown as innocents who have thus far been uncontaminated by the backwater views of adults.

A student in one New York City school thinks even 5- and 6-year-olds should be given books about the homosexual lifestyle. If parents "freak out," it's only because they are "biased." And a second grade boy in Cambridge, Mass., says an adult who is opposed to lesbianism is not very "open-minded," and in fact is downright "prejudiced." This theme supplies the rationale for It's Elementary: keep the discussion of homosexuality out of the hands of ignorant parents, and place it in the hands of an enlightened public school system.

CIRCUMVENTING PARENTS

Celia Klehr, whose child has gone through her school's pro-homosexual program, has nothing but praise for the curriculum. But what if a parent disapproves of homosexuality? The program is still beneficial, Klehr insists.

"At least this way it opens the topic," she says, "so that you can then teach what you believe to your child." But Klehr's reasoning begs the question—should schools be teaching this in the first place? If a parent views homosexuality as wrong, what is the child to do with a contradictory message coming from another respected authority figure—the child's teacher? A wedge has been driven between the child's two worlds: home and school; doubt has been raised in the child's mind about whether or not his/her parents are wrong.

What if a child simply accepts the teacher's pro-gay view without question, and never raises the issue at home? The moral values of some parents have been effectively undermined by an authority figure at school, and homosexual advocates have won the initial skirmish in the war for the hearts and minds of a future generation. . . .

Perhaps one of the most shocking statements in It's Elementary came from Thomas Price, principal of Cambridge Friends School in Cambridge, Mass. "I don't think that it's appropriate that values only be taught at home," he said. "There are social values as well, there are community values." And apparently those critical community values include this one: homosexuality is good.

PUBLIC SCHOOL ADVOCACY OF GAY ISSUES

The underlying belief of these social architects is that parents cannot be trusted to convey the truth about homosexuality to their children. The intervention of the public schools is necessary. At a faculty meeting at Cambridge Friends School, the teachers are discussing the results of their fourth annual Gay and Lesbian Pride Day. One teacher admits, "I think that we are asking kids to believe that (the homosexual lifestyle) is right. . . . [W]e're educating them, and this is part of what we consider to be a healthy education."

Some go beyond mere recommendation of advocacy. Take for example George Sloan, principal at Luther Burbank Middle School in San Francisco. Sloan said he believed that learning under a pro-homosexual curricula "should be mandatory" for all students.

At the Manhattan Country School in New York City, eighth grade English teacher Carol O'Donnell listens as one student complains that she is confused about the issue of homosexuality, because her family tells her it's wrong.

Another student agrees that kids hear different things from different places. The solution? "[S]chool needs to give us all the facts, so we can decide on our own what to think and what to do."

Some parents might be disturbed to know that their voice has been relegated to the status of being one among many. Yet it is the opinion promulgated in It's Elementary that, when conflicting voices sow confusion, the public school system can intervene with the facts so the children can decide for themselves.

But are they given the facts? And are they really deciding for themselves?

THE MANIPULATION OF CHILDREN

The introduction to the video tries to calm parental fears, by assuring them that the pro-gay curricula in schools will only be presented in "an age-appropriate way." This translates very simply: rather than discussing sexual practices and sexually transmitted diseases, the teachers will frame the issue as a discussion about tolerance and civil rights.

In New York City's Public School 87, fourth grade teacher Cora Sangree is reminding her students of a previous assignment, when she told them to paint whatever came to mind when she said the word, "Indian." Now, she tells her children, they are to write whatever comes to mind when she says the word "lesbian" and "gay."

One student asks, "So nothing's right or wrong in this either?" "That's right," Sangree replies. "There's no right or wrong answer."

Those words play well to the casual observer of It's Elementary. But a more critical examination of the video shows teachers' subtle but powerful manipulation of the children to draw the desired conclusion.

GAY RIGHTS PROPAGANDA

In one scene from the video It's Elementary: Talking About Gay Issues in School, a fifth grader explains how the Nazis used pink triangles to distinguish homosexuals to put them in concentration camps. Another fifth grader remarks, "Some Christians believe that if you're gay, you'll go to hell, so they want to torture them and stuff like that." Biblical admonitions about homosexuality are either ignored or misconstrued. The only reasonable view presented is total acceptance of homosexuality, with any resistance portrayed as bigotry.

Robert H. Knight, Weekly Standard, April 7, 1997.

In Kate Lyman's first/second grade class the students often do "class books," put together by the students themselves. On this day, Lyman shows the class their latest finished project, entitled, "Everybody is Equal: A Book About Gays and Lesbians." The computer-generated introduction to their book says, in part, "We made this book to tell people to respect gay and lesbian people . . ." The teacher thus established the parameters of acceptable viewpoints in advance of the project: if you don't think homosexuality is "equal" to heterosexuality, you don't "respect" gay people.

At one school assembly celebrating Gay and Lesbian Pride Day, a teacher stands before the students and tells them he's gay. Another teacher tearfully tells the children how proud she is of what they are doing, and encourages them to change the world with what they've learned.

At the beginning of It's Elementary, the narrator explained, "We made this film to explore what does happen when experienced teachers talk about lesbians and gay men with their students." What happens is clear. The sight of teachers standing before the entire school body in support of homosexuality has a coercive influence upon children that is frightening.

Later Sangree, alone with the camera, discusses her observations about the day's teaching session. The children, she says, are getting a lot of "misinformation" about homosexuals—not only from the culture, but also parents. And, she says, apparently to defuse potential protests, the curriculum does not talk about sex. That, she says, would be inappropriate. Instead, the school is merely attempting to eliminate "stereotypes" and promote respect. "[T]alking about people in different communities, and biases and discrimination and how that affects people's lives," Sangree said, "I think is appropriate."

Here, finally, we discover that there is indeed a right and wrong answer after all.

STACKING THE DECK

If some of the teachers do not explicitly say that people are wrong when they oppose homosexuality, they do so implicitly. The words "gays and lesbians" are circled on the chalkboard in the third grade class of teacher Daithi Wolfe, at Hawthorne Elementary School in Madison, Wisconsin. Then, as he begins to write down the words that students associate with homosexuality, a curious pattern develops. Any negative words offered by students about homosexuals are placed on the right side of his circle: "Homophobia." "Discrimination." "Name-calling." "Weird." And, of course, "Nazis" and "Hitler."

But on the left side of the board—apparently the side with the "right" words—are "pink triangle," "rainbow necklace," "same (as real people)," and "equal rights." Such blatant manipulation might not work on adults, but it is clearly effective on children.

Kim Coates, an eighth grade health science teacher at Luther Burbank Middle School in San Francisco, invited two homosexuals to address her class. One of the speakers, a lesbian, starts off telling the students that she didn't come to school to recruit kids into the homosexual lifestyle. Instead, she admits that she came to change their minds about gays. While they may have come to school thinking homosexuals are evil, she hoped they would leave thinking that "gay people are just like me."

And she accomplishes her goal. After the class, some of the students are interviewed, and they admit that the two speakers have changed the way they view homosexuality.

A SKEWED VIEW OF CHRISTIANITY

When It's Elementary is not pointing the finger at bigoted parents in general, it zeroes in on Christians in particular: the Christian view of homosexuality is highlighted as an example of outrageous bigotry. In one sequence of clips from TV talk shows, two apparent Christians present the view of their faith. One says, "God hates fags." The other: "The Bible that I read says homosexuals should be put to death."

Later, a fifth grade boy observes, "Some Christians believe that if you're gay or lesbian that you'll go to hell, so they want to torture them." This skewed view of Christianity is no accident. Chasnoff has said that the film was made, in part, to counter the "hysteria of the Religious Right." But not all religious views of homosexuality are ridiculed in the video. What, for example, is the theological position of Thomas Price, principal of Cambridge Friends School? "We really believe that there's God in every person, and those people include homosexuals, too," he says. In a twist that is positively evil, the children at one Gay and Lesbian Pride Day school assembly are led by a platoon of teachers in singing, "This Little Light of Mine."

If there was any doubt remaining, the moral worldview of the pro-homosexual curricula surveyed in It's Elementary is clarified by one teacher in Cambridge.

After saying that students must be taught that all lifestyles are equal, she says, "There isn't a right way, there isn't a wrong way; there isn't a good way, there isn't a bad way. The way that it is, is what it is."

Homosexual advocates have realized that their greatest potential for changing America's mind about the gay lifestyle lies in changing the seed for tomorrow's crop. . . . With efforts like It's Elementary, homosexuals are well on their way to deciding what that tomorrow will look like.

VIEWPOINT

7

|"We should stop telling young people
and others struggling with
homosexuality that they're stuck
with it. Instead we should say, 'If
you want to change, you [can], like
so many others who have.'"

THERAPISTS SHOULD HELP PEOPLE OVERCOME UNWANTED HOMOSEXUALITY

National Association for Research and Therapy of Homosexuality

The National Association for Research and Therapy of Homosexuality (NARTH) is an information and referral network for people interested in changing unwanted homosexuality through psychological treatment. In the following viewpoint, NARTH contends that homosexuals who would like to become heterosexual can do so with the help of psychological therapy. Research proves that years of intense therapy have helped a majority of survey respondents to overcome unwanted homosexuality, NARTH maintains. Such results, the organization argues, prove that homosexuality is a psychological and not a biological or genetic condition.

As you read, consider the following questions:

1. According to the research conducted by NARTH, what percentage of survey respondents became either exclusively or almost entirely heterosexual after undergoing therapy to change their sexual orientation?
2. What percentage of surveyed psychologists believe that homosexuals can become heterosexual, according to NARTH?

Reprinted from National Association for Research and Therapy of Homosexuality, "New Study Confirms Homosexuality Can Be Overcome," NARTH Bulletin, August 1997, with permission of NARTH.

N early 25 years after the American Psychiatric Association officially removed homosexuality from its Diagnostic Manual, labeling it a lifestyle choice rather than a psychological disorder, a California-based association of psychiatrists and psychologists has proven that homosexuals can change their orientation through intense therapy and a strong desire to change.

The National Association for Research and Therapy of Homosexuality (NARTH) released the results of a two-year study in May 1997 in conjunction with its annual meeting of licensed psychologists and psychotherapists, social workers, family counselors, clergy and related professionals. The study was conducted among nearly 860 individuals struggling to overcome homosexuality and more than 200 psychologists and therapists who treat them. The survey was sponsored by NARTH; its data was tabulated by professionals at Brigham Young University.

"This research proves, once and for all, that a degree of sexual-orientation change is possible," said Dr. Joseph Nicolosi, a psychologist and executive director of NARTH. "We should stop telling young people and others struggling with homosexuality that they're stuck with it. Instead we should say, 'If you want to change, you may be able to, like so many others who have.'"

The Findings of the Survey

The survey was conducted among individuals who were previously thought to be non-existent as a population; this study demonstrates that such individuals do exist.

Among the study's significant findings is a documented shift in respondents' sexual orientation, as well as the frequency and intensity of their homosexual thoughts and actions. Specifically, the survey indicated:

- Before treatment, 68 percent of respondents perceived themselves as exclusively or almost entirely homosexual, with another 22 percent stating they were more homosexual than heterosexual. After treatment, only 13 percent perceived themselves as exclusively or almost entirely homosexual, while 33 percent described themselves as either exclusively or almost entirely heterosexual.
- Although 83 percent of respondents indicated that they entered therapy primarily because of homosexuality, 99 percent of those who participated in the survey said they now believe treatment to change homosexuality can be effective and valuable.

- As a group, those surveyed reported statistically significant decreases following treatment in the frequency and intensity of their homosexual thoughts, in the frequency of masturbation to gay pornography, and in the frequency of their homosexual behavior with a partner. Respondents also indicated that, as a result of treatment and sexual orientation changes, they were also improving psychologically and interpersonally.
- Of the psychotherapists surveyed, 82 percent said they believe therapy can help change unwanted homosexuality. They further indicated that on average, one-third to one-half of their patients had adopted a primarily heterosexual orientation.
- And more than 95 percent of the psychotherapists said they either strongly agreed or somewhat agreed with the statement that homosexual patients may be capable of changing to a heterosexual orientation.

HOMOSEXUALITY IS PSYCHOLOGICAL

At the time of the survey, 63 percent of participants indicated that they were still in treatment, having spent an average of three and one-third years (or 42 sessions) in therapy up to that point. Of the primarily Caucasian sample, 78 percent were men, 22 percent were women, with an average age of 37. Over half of the participants had never been married, and approximately one-third were married. Almost 90 percent of the survey's respondents had a college education.

"Clearly this research validates homosexuality as a psychological condition, rather than a genetic or hereditary one," said Nicolosi, adding that studies that have found correlations with genetic factors indicate *predisposition*, not *causation*. "As a result," he continued, "we must not turn our backs on those individuals who want to find a way out of homosexuality."

COMMENTS OF SURVEY RESPONDENTS

A qualitative portion of the survey confirmed Nicolosi's statements. Comments provided by respondents included:

- "When I realized that homosexuality was a trap," one man stated, "I turned to others for help. My therapist and our relationship provided a model for appropriate male-to-male, nonsexual relationships, and taught me about appropriate touching, bonding and expression of needs."
- Another man wrote: "I had been involved in compulsive behavior several times a week for eight years, from the time I

REPARATIVE THERAPY IS A PROCESS

Growth through reparative therapy is in one way like the gay model of coming out of the closet. That is, it is an ongoing process. Usually some homosexual desires will persist or recur during certain times in the life cycle.

Therefore, rather than "cure," we refer to the goal of "change," a meaning shift beginning with a change in identification of self. As one married ex-gay man described it: "For many years I thought I was gay. I finally realized I was not a homosexual, but really a heterosexual man with a homosexual problem."

Joseph Nicolosi, *Reparative Therapy of Male Homosexuality*, 1991.

---

left home and began living on my own. I had occasional physical encounters as well. Since joining a therapy group, I've had no recurrence of compulsive masturbation, no use of phone sex or pornography, with basically no desire to participate in those behaviors. The attraction to men lingers, but every week I participate [in] the group encourages me more."

- A female respondent stated: "I never expected this much recovery. My relationships with men have greatly improved—I am able to relate sexually to my husband in a way I was never able to before. I'm learning to leave the familiar protective emotions of contempt, arrogance, pseudo self-sufficiency, anger and self-indulgence behind, and practice the emotions of love instead."

- "Change is extremely difficult and requires total commitment," said a male respondent. "But I have broken the terrible power that homosexuality had over me for so long. I haven't been this light and happy since I was a child. People can and do change, and become free."

A NEW VOICE

"NARTH will give a new voice to these individuals and the hundreds more who participated in our study," Nicolosi said, indicating that his organization intends to disseminate the survey's results to leaders in the religious, political and scientific communities. "As professionals, we cannot allow the American public to be deceived one minute longer. We must be allowed to reach out to those who want our help and help them. And we intend to continue to do so."

MAKING THERAPY AVAILABLE

Founded in 1992, NARTH exists to make effective psychological therapy available to all homosexual men and women who seek change, primarily through referral services in the U.S. and abroad. Among the nonprofit organization's members are leading psychologists who lecture and publish regularly on the subject of homosexuality, its causes and its treatment. Its membership is open to all who share its ideals.

"Homosexual orientation is not a
mental illness and there is no
scientific reason to attempt
conversion of lesbians or gays to
heterosexual orientation."

THERAPISTS SHOULD NOT TRY TO CHANGE ANYONE'S SEXUAL ORIENTATION

American Psychological Association

The American Psychological Association (APA) is an organization that works to advance psychology as a science, as a profession, and as a means of promoting human welfare. In the following viewpoint, the APA contends that homosexuality is not a mental disorder and that therapists should not attempt to change a gay person's sexual orientation. Reports that have concluded that gays and lesbians can successfully "convert" to heterosexuality are biased and unscientific, the APA asserts. Rather than promoting alleged gay conversion therapy, mental health providers should work to dispel the myth that homosexuality is abnormal and to eliminate antigay prejudice and discrimination, maintains the APA.

As you read, consider the following questions:

1. According to the American Psychological Association, what are the four components of sexuality?
2. Why was homosexuality considered a mental illness in the past, according to the APA?
3. Who has the most favorable attitudes toward gays and lesbians, according to the APA?

W*hat is sexual orientation?*
Sexual orientation is one of the four components of sexuality and is distinguished by an enduring emotional, romantic, sexual or affectionate attraction to individuals of a particular gender. The three other components of sexuality are biological sex, gender identity (the psychological sense of being male or female) and social sex role (adherence to cultural norms for feminine and masculine behavior). Three sexual orientations are commonly recognized: homosexual, attraction to individuals of one's own gender; heterosexual, attraction to individuals of the other gender; or bisexual, attractions to members of either gender. Persons with a homosexual orientation are sometimes referred to as gay (both men and women) or as lesbian (women only).

Sexual orientation is different from sexual behavior because it refers to feelings and self-concept. Persons may or may not express their sexual orientation in their behaviors.

THE CAUSES OF HOMOSEXUALITY

What causes a person to have a particular sexual orientation?

How a particular sexual orientation develops in any individual is not well understood by scientists. Various theories have proposed differing sources for sexual orientation, including genetic or inborn hormonal factors and life experiences during early childhood. However, many scientists share the view that sexual orientation is shaped for most people at an early age through complex interactions of biological, psychological and social factors.

Is sexual orientation a choice?

No. Sexual orientation emerges for most people in early adolescence without any prior sexual experience. And some people report trying very hard over many years to change their sexual orientation from homosexual to heterosexual with no success. For these reasons, psychologists do not consider sexual orientation for most people to be a conscious choice that can be voluntarily changed.

Is homosexuality a mental illness or emotional problem?

No. Psychologists, psychiatrists and other mental health professionals agree that homosexuality is not an illness, mental disorder or emotional problem. Much objective scientific research over the past 35 years shows us that homosexual orientation, in and of itself, is not associated with emotional or social problems.

Homosexuality was thought to be a mental illness in the past because mental health professionals and society had biased information about homosexuality since most studies only involved lesbians and gay men in therapy. When researchers examined data about gay people who were not in therapy, the idea that homosexuality was a mental illness was found to be untrue.

In 1973 the American Psychiatric Association confirmed the importance of the new research by removing the term 'homosexuality' from the official manual that lists all mental and emotional disorders. In 1975 the American Psychological Association passed a resolution supporting this action. Both associations urge all mental health professionals to help dispel the stigma of mental illness that some people still associate with homosexual orientation. Since the original declassification of homosexuality as a mental disorder, this decision has subsequently been reaffirmed by additional research findings and both associations.

Can lesbians and gay men be good parents?

Yes. Studies comparing groups of children raised by homosexual and by heterosexual parents find no developmental differences between the two groups of children in their intelligence, psychological adjustment, social adjustment, popularity with friends, development of social sex role identity or development of sexual orientation.

Another stereotype about homosexuality is the mistaken belief that gay men have more of a tendency than heterosexual men to sexually molest children. There is no evidence indicating that homosexuals are more likely than heterosexuals to molest children.

Gay and Lesbian Identity Development

Why do some gay men and lesbians tell people about their sexual orientation?

Because sharing that aspect of themselves with others is important to their mental health. In fact, the process of identity development for lesbians and gay men, usually called 'coming out', has been found to be strongly related to psychological adjustment—the more positive the gay male or lesbian identity, the better one's mental health and the higher one's self-esteem.

Why is the 'coming out' process difficult for some gays and lesbians?

Because of false stereotypes and unwarranted prejudice towards them, the process of 'coming out' for lesbians and gay men can be a very challenging process which may cause emotional pain. Lesbian and gay people often feel 'different' and alone when they first become aware of same-sex attractions. They may also fear being rejected by family, friends, co-workers and religious institutions if they do 'come out'.

In addition, homosexuals are frequently the targets of discrimination and violence. This threat of violence and discrimination is an obstacle to lesbian and gay people's development. In a 1989 national survey, 5% of the gay men and 10% of the lesbians reported physical abuse or assault related to being lesbian or gay in the last year; 47% reported some form of discrimination over their lifetime. Other research has shown similarly high rates of discrimination or violence.

A Statement on Reparative Therapy

There is no published scientific evidence supporting the efficacy of 'reparative therapy' as a treatment to change one's sexual orientation. . . . There are a few reports in the literature of efforts to use psychotherapeutic and counseling techniques to treat persons troubled by their homosexuality who desire to become heterosexual; however, results have not been conclusive, nor have they been replicated. There is no evidence that any treatment can change a homosexual person's deep seated sexual feelings for others of the same sex. Clinical experience suggests that any person who seeks conversion therapy may be doing so because of social bias that has resulted in internalized homophobia, and that gay men and lesbians who have accepted their sexual orientation positively are better adjusted than those who have not done so.

American Psychiatric Association, on-line report, January 1996.

What can be done to help lesbians and gay men overcome prejudice and discrimination against them?

The people who have the most positive attitudes toward gay men and lesbians are those who say they know one or more gay persons well. For this reason, psychologists believe negative attitudes toward gays as a group are prejudices that are not grounded in actual experience with lesbians or gay men but on stereotypes and prejudice.

Furthermore, protection against violence and discrimination are very important, just as they are for other minority groups. Some states include violence against an individual on the basis of her or his sexual orientation as a 'hate crime' and eight U.S. states have laws against discrimination on the basis of sexual orientation.

Therapy and Sexual Orientation

Can therapy change sexual orientation?

No. Even though homosexual orientation is not a mental illness and there is no scientific reason to attempt conversion of lesbians or gays to heterosexual orientation, some individuals may seek to change their own sexual orientation or that of another individual (for example, parents seeking therapy for their child). Some therapists who undertake this kind of therapy report that they have changed their client's sexual orientation (from homosexual to heterosexual) in treatment. Close scrutiny of their reports indicates several factors that cast doubt: many of the claims come from organizations with an ideological perspective on sexual orientation, rather than from mental health researchers; the treatments and their outcomes are poorly documented; and the length of time that clients are followed up after the treatment is too short.

In 1990, the American Psychological Association stated that scientific evidence does not show that conversion therapy works and that it can do more harm than good. Changing one's sexual orientation is not simply a matter of changing one's sexual behavior. It would require altering one's emotional, romantic and sexual feelings and restructuring one's self-concept and social identity. Although some mental health providers do attempt sexual orientation conversion, others question the ethics of trying to alter through therapy a trait that is not a disorder and that is extremely important to an individual's identity.

Not all gays and lesbians who seek therapy want to change their sexual orientation. Gays and lesbians may seek counseling for any of the same reasons as anyone else. In addition, they may need psychological help to 'come out' or to deal with prejudice, discrimination and violence.

Why is it important for society to be better educated about homosexuality?

Educating all people about sexual orientation and homosexuality is likely to diminish anti-gay prejudice. Accurate information about homosexuality is especially important to young people struggling with their own sexual identity. Fears that access to such information will affect one's sexual orientation are not valid.

PERIODICAL BIBLIOGRAPHY

The following articles have been selected to supplement the diverse views presented in this chapter. Addresses are provided for periodicals not indexed in the *Readers' Guide to Periodical Literature*, the *Alternative Press Index*, the *Social Sciences Index*, or the *Index to Legal Periodicals and Books*.

Norma J. Bailey and Tracy Phariss	"Gay Students in Middle School," *Education Digest*, October 1996.
William J. Bennett	"Clinton, Gays, and the Truth," *Weekly Standard*, November 24, 1997. Available from News America Publishing, Inc., 1211 Avenue of the Americas, New York, NY 10036.
Commonweal	"Our Children: Bishops' Statement to Parents of Gays," November 21, 1997.
Joshua Gamson	"Do Ask, Do Tell," *American Prospect*, Fall 1995.
Henry Gonshak	"Coming Out of the Celluloid Closet," *Peace Review*, March 1996.
Laurie Goodstein	"The Architect of the 'Gay Conversion' Campaign," *New York Times*, August 13, 1998.
David Lipsky	"To Be Young and Gay," *Rolling Stone*, August 6, 1998.
Mark Miller	"Going to War over Gays," *Newsweek*, July 27, 1998.
Mark Peyser	"Battling Backlash," *Newsweek*, August 17, 1998.
Patrick G.D. Riley	"Homosexuality and the Maccabean Revolt," *New Oxford Review*, September 1997. Available from 1069 Kains Ave., Berkeley, CA 94706-2260.
Eric Rofes	"Gay Issues, Schools, and the Right-Wing Backlash," *Rethinking Schools*, Spring 1997.
Thomas Storck	"Is Opposition to Homosexual Activity 'Irrational'?" *New Oxford Review*, May 1997.
Alan Wolfe	"The Homosexual Exception," *New York Times Magazine*, February 8, 1998.
David Yegerlehner	"Genesis 19: Taking the Offensive," *Harvard Gay & Lesbian Review*, Fall 1996.

CHAPTER 4

SHOULD SOCIETY SANCTION GAY AND LESBIAN FAMILIES?

CHAPTER PREFACE

Most cultures have defined marriage as a lifelong union between a man and a woman. In the early 1990s, however, three same-sex couples challenged Hawaii's marriage statute in court, claiming that sanctioning only heterosexual unions was a form of sex discrimination. The ensuing controversy surrounding the possibility of same-sex marriage has generated heated debate.

Many opponents of same-sex marriage argue that the trend toward acceptance of openly gay couples is an affront to traditional family values. Legalizing gay marriage, they contend, would allow America to condone an immoral lifestyle and would wrongly demand its citizens—the majority of whom do not approve of homosexuality—to acknowledge same-sex partnerships as viable family units. Some critics of gay marriage are especially concerned about same-sex couples having children through adoption or reproductive technology. In the opinion of Bradley P. Hayton, a former research analyst with the Family Research Council, "Homosexuals cannot meet the psychological, emotional, spiritual, social, and educational needs of children. . . . Homosexuality is physically and emotionally abnormal, and thus trains children in behaviors and virtues that are destructive to the social fabric."

Supporters of gay marriage, however, maintain that same-sex couples should have access to the same rights that heterosexual spouses have—namely, the public recognition of the seriousness and depth of their relationships. Many proponents believe, moreover, that sanctioning gay marriage would actually strengthen the family by allowing more couples to enter into stable, long-term, lawful unions. In time, these supporters argue, same-sex marriage would help integrate gays and lesbians into mainstream culture and destroy the stereotype of homosexuality as abnormal or immoral behavior. Breaking down such stereotypes, argues lesbian psychologist April Martin, would enable society to understand that gay parents are not a threat to children: "We lesbians and gay men choose to become parents for the same reasons heterosexuals do: to impart our love, our knowledge and our heritages to our children and to experience the joy of helping a young heart and mind develop. Ultimately, we desire to fulfill some of what is best in humanity."

The following chapter further explores this controversy over the viability of gay and lesbian families.

| "Many gay and lesbian couples want to make it clear to everyone that they have a relationship of the same general kind as society expects of married couples."

SOCIETY SHOULD ALLOW SAME-SEX MARRIAGE

Ralph Wedgwood

In the following viewpoint, Ralph Wedgwood argues that same-sex couples should have the right to marry. From marriage, he maintains, couples obtain more than legal benefits—they also gain the public acknowledgment that their relationship is a committed, long-term partnership. Even though much of society does not approve of gay relationships, Wedgwood contends, committed same-sex couples should have the opportunity to choose marriage as a means to convey the significance and seriousness of their relationships. Wedgwood is an assistant professor of philosophy at the Massachusetts Institute of Technology in Cambridge.

As you read, consider the following questions:

1. According to Wedgwood, what are some of the mutual rights and obligations of married couples?
2. What are society's shared expectations of marriage, according to the author?
3. In Wedgwood's opinion, why are domestic partnerships ineffective at conveying the seriousness of long-term relationships?

Reprinted from Ralph Wedgwood, "What Are We Fighting For?" *The Harvard Gay and Lesbian Review*, Fall 1997, with permission.

The same-sex marriage debate raises some difficult questions. Is same-sex marriage really worth fighting for? What would same-sex marriage mean for us? What exactly is marriage anyway?

Many advocates of same-sex marriage seem to assume that marriage is a purely legal institution, consisting of a cluster of legal rights, obligations, and benefits. Married couples have mutual rights and obligations, such as the right to mutual financial support and (in the event of divorce or separation) to alimony and an equitable division of property; and they also receive certain state-provided benefits such as tax breaks, preferential immigration treatment, tenancy succession rights, health insurance benefits, and so on.

If marriage is no more than this, however, then it is not marriage itself that matters, but only its constituent rights and benefits. But the best way to secure these rights and benefits for same-sex couples may not be to try to get them through "marriage" as such. After all, the mutual rights and obligations of marriage can already be re-created by means of private contracts, wills, and power-of-attorney agreements. And some of the other legal benefits of marriage are already being split off from marriage and provided to same-sex couples. Even though same-sex marriage does not exist anywhere in the world, same-sex partners already receive health insurance benefits from many employers, preferential immigration treatment from some countries, tenancy succession rights in some cities, and so on. If these legal rights and benefits are all that matter, then it is probably a mistake to try to secure them all at once by fighting for full same-sex marriage.

MARRIAGE IS MORE THAN RIGHTS AND BENEFITS

As most people intuitively sense, however, marriage is more than just a cluster of legal rights and benefits. Of course the legal aspects of marriage are important. But marriage involves more than this. Marriage is a fusion of law and culture. It is a legal status that not only confers legal rights and obligations, but also has crucial effects on how the married couple is regarded by society.

The point is not that the law requires or encourages people to approve of and support the married couple's relationship—the law does nothing to deter me from disapproving of a friend's marriage, or even from persuading my friend to get divorced, if I see fit to do so—but that society as a whole has certain *generally shared expectations* about the kind of relationship that married couples typically have (while it lacks any such clear expectations about relationships of other sorts). Once a couple is legally married, society will come to expect that their relationship is of this kind. These expectations include, at least in our society, that the couple engage in intimacy and probably sex; that they have shared finances and a shared household, or at least co-operate extensively in coping with the necessities of life; that they have a serious long-term commitment to their relationship; and that the relationship involves certain legal rights and obligations, notably the right to mutual financial support.

The Legal Aspects of Marriage

The legal aspects of marriage complement and undergird society's shared expectations of marriage. Marriage is a legal status: the question "Is Chris married to Jo?" is a legal question; it is the law that determines who is married and who is not. This means that there is general agreement about who is married and who is not, thus allowing the married couple to be regarded as married by society as a whole (not just by their particular circle or subculture). The legally binding mutual rights and obligations of marriage reflect society's expectations of marriage, and when necessary are enforced, thus providing an assurance that these expectations will be fulfilled. For example, rights such as the right to spousal support and (in the event of divorce or separation) to alimony and an equitable division of property reinforce the generally shared expectation that marriage involves a serious mutual commitment to long-term economic and domestic partnership. In this way, these legal aspects of marriage, together with the fact that marriage is so familiar, provide an assurance that society as a whole will share these generally shared expectations of marriage, and that the married couple's relationship will be regarded in the light of these expectations.

This helps to explain what attracts couples to the institution of marriage. Couples get married because they not only want to make a legally binding commitment to each other, but also want to get the rest of society to understand that they have a serious commitment to an intimate relationship, which involves long-term domestic and economic partnership. It is the public recognition of the status of "married" that constitutes the most important benefit of marriage, and what is most crucially abridged when the State discriminates against gay couples who want to marry.

Same-Sex Commitments Are Serious

Same-sex couples want to get married for the same reasons that heterosexual couples do. They not only want the legal rights and benefits of marriage; they also want to be regarded as married by society. It is all too easy for the rest of society to ignore same-sex relationships, and to assume that they are only sexual, or involve no serious long-term commitment or sharing of finances and household responsibilities. Many gay and lesbian couples want to make it clear to everyone that they have a relationship of the same general kind as society expects of married couples. Domestic partnerships are just less effective for this purpose. If you say, "Chris and I are domestic partners," your audience may wonder, "Do domestic partnerships expire every month unless they are renewed? Are the partners obliged to support each other financially? Do they have a sexual relationship—or are they just roommates who want to keep the rent-controlled apartment if the other dies?" For society at large, domestic partnerships and commitment ceremonies are less familiar than marriage; they lack the resonance of marriage.

Reprinted by permission of John Branch.

Same-sex marriage would clearly not deprive anyone else of any important benefits of marriage, and would not fundamentally change its definition (intimacy, shared household, mutual commitment, and so on). Other elements that may be included in this definition, such as procreation, are far from being as categorical as the ones I've specified. Thus, for example, while there may be a general expectation that many couples will have children together, society has never expected *all* married couples to do so.

Some opponents of same-sex marriage are concerned that if marriage were extended to couples who *obviously* cannot procreate together, this would weaken the association between marriage and procreation, reducing married couples' motivation to have children. Others worry that same-sex marriages would be more liable to marital breakdown than heterosexual marriages, but this is mere speculation in the absence of any accumulated experience with same-sex marriage.

GAY MARRIAGE IS WORTH FIGHTING FOR

The ban on same-sex marriage certainly cannot be justified on the grounds that it serves to express and reinforce the view, which a number of people hold, that heterosexual unions are superior to homosexual unions, based on religious credos or moral statements. The State cannot justify its actions by appeal to such controversial moral or religious views, any more than it can justify them by appeal to the view that Christianity is superior to Judaism. The ban on same-sex marriage is opposed by some because it seems to install homosexual relations as equal in value to heterosexual ones. Technically, it does no such thing. The state allows convicted wife-murderers, child-abusers, and rapists to marry, even while in jail; it is not expressing any sort of approval of these relationships.

Once we understand what marriage is, we can see what marriage would mean for us, and why it is worth fighting for. Same-sex marriage would not force anyone to honor or approve of gay or lesbian relationships against their will. But it would enable those of us who are involved in gay or lesbian relationships to get the rest of society to understand that we take these relationships just as seriously as heterosexual married couples take theirs. And without marriage, we remain second-class citizens—excluded, for no good reason, from participating in one of the basic institutions of society.

| "Homosexual marriage would further
weaken an already-damaged
institution, to the detriment of us
all—homosexuals included."

SOCIETY SHOULD NOT ALLOW SAME-SEX MARRIAGE

Burman Skrable

Legalizing same-sex marriage would be harmful to society, argues Burman Skrable in the following viewpoint. He contends that the primary goal of marriage is the bearing and raising of children, who are vital to the future stability of society. The sexual revolution, however, has weakened the institution of marriage by attacking the bonds between marriage, sex, and children, Skrable maintains. Homosexual marriage, he concludes, would further damage marriage and the family by legitimizing a dangerous kind of nonprocreative sexual behavior and lifestyle. Skrable is a freelance writer and a quality control officer for the U.S. Department of Labor.

As you read, consider the following questions:
1. What is the "original school for children," according to the author?
2. In Skrable's opinion, which nationwide legal reforms have damaged marriage and the family?
3. What is the contemporary definition of marriage, according to Skrable?

Excerpted from Burman Skrable, "Homosexual Marriage: Much to Fear," Culture Wars, October 1996, by permission of Culture Wars.

In defense of . . . Christians who have tried to respond to the demand for same-sex marriage from their religious beliefs, it should be noted that this is not the first time an institution or doctrine which has been unquestioningly accepted for aeons is suddenly challenged, and whose defenders found themselves grasping, at first ineffectively, for an appropriate response. In fact, history is full of similar instances, although our era may be the most "challenged." We live in an age which can almost be defined by its proclivity for questioning practically every received doctrine and belief, and by the way our dominant attitude-shaping institutions have shifted the benefit of the doubt from the defenders of the status quo to its challengers. This shift in the burden of proof has undoubtedly helped ensure the success of the sexual revolution, which has systematically challenged the rationale for one thing connected with sex after another. That said, however, it is definitely high time, if not too late, to catch up with the need for an effective response. Much rides on it.

We need to move the foundation of our argument from the religious to the scientific. The validity of many of the tenets of our Christian beliefs have been well proved by the social sciences. Thus, there is nothing particularly religious about the argument I propose. Its main premise is that societies have a life-and-death interest in ensuring their own survival, and thus a responsibility to act to further that interest. The importance of this approach was acknowledged, although not developed, by Cardinal Bernard Law. Queried by the *National Catholic Register* in Portland, Oregon, in the summer of 1996, about the Hawaii case, the cardinal said "The issue is—what is marriage? What's the State's interest in marriage?" [The Hawaii case—*Baehr v. Miike*—resulted in a ruling that the prohibition of same-sex marriage is unconstitutional. The case was appealed to the Hawaii Supreme Court, and a decision was expected in late 1998.] . . .

THE TRADITIONAL FAMILY

To remain vital, every society must ensure stability in the present and provide for its future. Everyone, including the homosexually oriented, depends on these things being done, and done well. The two objectives are closely related, and children are at the focus of both. Providing for the future means bearing, educating and socializing children; children are our social security, economically, physically and emotionally. If there are not enough of them, there will eventually be a disproportion between those able to work and those who cannot, and the burden of supporting the dependent population can become so severe that it strains society's bonds. If the children are not raised properly, the well-being of those who depend on them later is threatened as much as, if not more than, if there are too few children.

Marriage provides for society's future by formally constituting the family. The traditional family—husband, wife, and natural children—is the only way societies have ever found of providing well for stability in the present and for our future. The family is the first community, the original unit which precedes and forms the basis of all larger and subsequent units. It is the original school for children, where they are taught all the values and mores that form them in how they interact, first with one another, and later with others to whom they are not related. It is irreplaceable in that it is a community of love, a community based on love; what parents do for children out of love cannot be replicated in a setting where the same tasks are done for pay.

As all who have undertaken the task of raising a family—and those who merely observe with detachment—will agree, it is an awesome and difficult business. For a couple to bear and raise children, and often even to stay together, is hard work and expensive. In its own interest, society must do what it can to ease those burdens and reward what is so central to its stability and continuation. By easing some of the financial burden and elevating the stature of the family, society hopes to induce its citizens to follow in the footsteps of their parents and grandparents and form families.

THE KIND OF MARRIAGE SOCIETY NEEDS

Marriage can thus be seen as a formal institution structured by society to help it meet its needs for stability in the present and continued existence over time. In marriage, a couple makes a formal, public commitment to one another to live as a single unit; the community endorses and ratifies that commitment. It also extends special recognition and usually various financial privileges to couples making this commitment. Its reason for doing so, as noted above, is its expectation that the couple will form a family unit, to bear and raise properly the children the society needs. Society's interest in all this is the children, period. Aside from the expectation of child-bearing and child raising, it has no strong interest in making marriage a privileged institution. . . .

The traditional understanding of marriage, and of the family that results from it, lines up perfectly to provide for the key needs identified above. Marriage once meant a permanent bond, the only approved locus for sex (i.e., marriage both establishes an exclusive sexual relationship and only the marriage relationship legitimizes sexual activity), and children. It went without saying that it was a man-woman relationship. Males and females have a natural complementarity in the process not only of procreating but also of raising children, and children thrive in an atmosphere of stability and commitment. Children also need the role models of both father and mother for their complete development. The atmosphere of stable commitment also helps regulate all of society's rhythms.

WHAT MARRIAGE HAS BECOME

One would hardly recognize in today's marriage the institution which the previous section argues best meets society's needs for stability and continuation. The villain of the piece is the generations-old social experiment called the sexual revolution. It has gradually drained the content from marriage, and with it, the vitality of the family. The main thrust of the sexual revolution has been to enable adults to separate sex from children and relieve them of binding commitments to one another. I'm not enough of an historian to know which came first: trying to chicken out on our lifetime commitments to one another, or separating the egg from the sperm. Whatever the order, the sexual revolution attacked, and gradually weakened, the covalent bonds of the marriage-sex-children triad. No-fault divorce vitiated permanence; first contraception and then abortion made the connection between sex and children optional; respected marriage gurus touted "open marriage." With sex no longer meaning children, the institutional warrant for marriage was questionable, and hence the fashionability of "living together."

SOCIETY'S ATTITUDE TOWARD HOMOSEXUALITY

For better or for worse, millions of Americans, of all faiths, reject the notion that homosexual conduct is merely an "alternative lifestyle," no more objectionable and no less acceptable than the traditional heterosexual lifestyle. These Americans strive hard to raise their children to recognize that not all expressions of sexuality are morally equivalent. Extending legal recognition to same-sex unions is government's way of telling those children that their parents are wrong, that their priests, ministers and rabbis are wrong, that civilized societies throughout the millennia have been wrong. We respectfully submit that government has no business conveying that message.

David Zweibel, testimony before the Senate Committee on the Judiciary, July 11, 1996.

The sexual revolution attacked both the legal framework surrounding and protecting marriage and the family and the moral climate. On the legal front, Supreme Court decisions overturned laws against contraception and abortion, states liberalized laws regulating divorce, and various laws affecting homosexual behavior have been challenged. In addition, there is a movement to establish a "right" of open homosexuality. Morally, the legal climate, technology and media-led opinion have all greatly influenced society's approvals and disapprovals. Living together and voluntary single parenthood receive hardly a blink today, whereas families with more than two children can expect many arched eyebrows and the obligatory query "don't you know about birth control?". . . .

Homosexual "Marriage"?

The sexual revolution gradually brought us to the point where the complex fabric of laws and mores which together supported and sustained marriage and the family has largely been unravelled. We are beginning to see the effects on social behavior. More to the point, these changes have gradually eroded our understanding of what marriage is. No longer is marriage considered universally in the public mind as a permanent union; no longer is it considered to have any necessary connection to children; no longer does it universally bind to fidelity; and that sex should be reserved for it is today's unthinkable thought. Marriage has become a mere diaphanous thing. To liberal journalist Karen Murray, for example, it means a public declaration of "the mutual devotion between any pair of adults," a pledge of "support, loyalty protection of the partner's privacy" which "others are expected to honor and reinforce."

The evolutionary emptying of the concept of marriage, and the concomitant acceptance of homosexual relations—both products of the same revolutionary forces—largely explain the drive for homosexual "marriage." Who, homosexual or heterosexual, could conceive of same-sex "marriage" if marriage meant more than it does today? More than anything else, our increasing technical ability to sever the biological link between sex and children, and the contraceptive mentality that grew from it—the belief that to separate sex from its natural consequences was not only natural but a right—probably paved the way for tolerating homosexual relations. But tolerance is not the same thing as acceptance. And even though marriage may now be but a shadow of its former self, it still retains some power to make sexual activity legitimate. So, same-sex couples grasp at it even when so many heterosexual couples find it superfluous. They may not believe society needs the institution of marriage, but it would salve their consciences and help them hold their heads high in public.

MAKING MARRIAGE MEANINGLESS

In view of the foregoing, it is easier to see what extending marriage to same-sex couples would do to the institution of marriage.

1. It would remove marriage's sole original defining characteristic, that it is a union of one man and one woman.

2. Although it would not change much of what is left of marriage—because not much is left today—it would lock in the "gains" of the sexual revolution. That, by itself, is extremely serious: what society really needs is the restoration of marriage; same-sex marriage would continue marriage on its present search for the bottom. That would further solidify the notions that sex need not have a necessary connection to procreation, nor marriage to children. Similarly, it is hard to imagine that same-sex couples—especially males—would want to see marriage restored to being a permanent and exclusive union. Male homosexual relations are inherently so transitory that many gay activists opposed same-sex marriage on the grounds that it would be so restrictive of the gay lifestyle that failure would be virtually guaranteed. In short, marriage would be further solidified as a meaningless institution in which society has no inherent interest, unless one makes the leap (not uncommonly implied today) of saying that society's real interest is in making us all feel good by legitimating every conceivable choice.

Allowing homosexual marriage would further dilute the uniqueness of marriage by opening it to all who want it, regardless of their potential to fulfill an essential societal function. If a privilege is open to all, it is no longer a privilege. This great levelling process would further diminish the incentives to bear and raise children. Homosexual marriage is a chimera of the real thing on which society depends for its continuation and health. It would further reinforce the sexual revolution's notion—which is too strong already—that any connection between sex and children is purely optional. It sends the subliminal message that everything should be a matter of choice, that nothing is a given or need be permanent, and that sexual differences are imaginative fictions imposed through socialization. I believe that these effects are enough to fear from extending marriage to same-sex couples.

A NEW MORAL LOW

Although most of its proponents are reticent to elaborate on this, same-sex marriage would really represent a drop to a new societal or moral low, because it would represent society's formal endorsement of homosexual activity. By giving it the writ of marriage, society gives it the stamp of approval. As [essayist] Alexander Pope said of vice, "We first endure, then pity, then embrace." With homosexual activity, we are now probably somewhere between enduring and pitying; same-sex marriage would be the embrace. Thus would society endorse an activity which its true interest is in eliminating. The hazards to the public health which homosexual sex represents, from HIV infections on down, are well known. Same-sex marriage would only raise them. . . .

This viewpoint has been an attempt to show that there is a very real sociological argument against same-sex marriage that is neither religious nor a front for aversion to persons with homosexual attractions. There are serious public policy reasons for not only keeping marriage heterosexual as it is, but also for attempting to restore its former meaning. Homosexual marriage would further weaken an already-damaged institution, to the detriment of us all—homosexuals included.

I also have tried to show that the push for homosexual marriage, while serious, is best understood as a symptom of a larger and more serious problem with our understanding of sex and marriage. The underlying causes of this serious problem are deeply rooted within our collective consciousness, and involve the acceptance—often by many profamily stalwarts themselves—of the destructive premises of the sexual revolution. Rooting these premises will be anything but easy; for many, no legislative or judicial remedy is possible. Profamily groups are right to fight homosexual marriage, however; although it may be largely symptomatic, permitting it will only make things worse.

"Why aren't [gay people] allowed to express their love as humanely as they possibly can, along with the infertile and the elderly?"

THE ROMAN CATHOLIC CHURCH SHOULD SANCTION GAY MARRIAGE

Andrew Sullivan

The Roman Catholic Church has no legitimate reason to oppose gay marriage, contends Andrew Sullivan in the following viewpoint. Although the church explicitly sanctions loving, procreative marriages, it also expresses compassion for infertile and elderly couples by allowing them to marry even though they cannot produce children, he points out. Since people do not choose their sexual orientation, Sullivan argues, the church should extend its compassion to gays and lesbians by offering them the sacrament of marriage. Sullivan is senior editor of the weekly magazine *New Republic*. He is also the author of *Virtually Normal: An Argument About Homosexuality*.

As you read, consider the following questions:

1. According to Sullivan, what does the Roman Catholic Church believe to be the two core elements of a nonsinful sexual act?
2. What kinds of sexual acts are considered sinful by the church, according to the author?
3. According to Sullivan, what is the church's stance toward homosexuals?

Reprinted from Andrew Sullivan, "What You Do," *The New Republic*, March 18, 1996, by permission of *The New Republic*. Copyright 1996 by The New Republic.

"Andrew, it's not who you are. It is what you do!" Pat Buchanan yelled across the table. We were engaged in a typically subtle *Crossfire* debate on same-gender marriage. I'd expected the explosion, but it nevertheless surprised me. Only minutes before, off the air, Buchanan had been cooing over my new haircut. But at least he could distinguish, like any good Jesuit, between the sin and the sinner. It was when his mind drifted to thoughts of homosexual copulation that his mood violently swung.

Okay, Pat, let's talk copulation. It isn't only me that has a problem here.

IS HOMOSEXUALITY A VICE?

Buchanan's fundamental issue with "what homosexuals do" is that it's what he calls a "vice." (I'll leave aside the demeaning reduction of "what homosexuals do" to a sexual act.) Now, there's a clear meaning for a vice: it's something bad that a person freely chooses to do, like, say, steal. But Buchanan concedes that gay relations aren't quite like that; they are related to a deeper, "very powerful impulse," (his words) to commit them. So a homosexual is like a kleptomaniac who decides to steal. Kleptomania is itself an involuntary, blameless condition, hard to resist, but still repressible. Kleptomaniacs, in Buchanan's words, "have the capacity not to engage in those acts. They have free will."

So far, so persuasive. The question begged, of course, is why same-gender sexual acts are wrong in the first place. In the case of kleptomania it's a no-brainer: someone else is injured directly by your actions; they're robbed. But, in the case of homosexual acts, where two consenting adults are engaged in a private activity, it's not at all clear who the injured party is. Buchanan's concern with homosexual acts derives, of course, from the Roman Catholic Church. And the Church's teaching about homosexual sex is closely related to its teaching about the sinfulness of all sexual activity outside a loving, procreative Church marriage.

SEX AND SIN

The sexual act, the Church affirms, must have two core elements: a "procreative" element, the willingness to be open to the creation of new life; and a "unitive" element, the intent to affirm a loving, faithful union. In this, the Church doesn't single out homosexuals for condemnation. The sin of gay sex is no more and no less sinful on these grounds than masturbation, extramarital sex, marital sex with contraception, heterosexual oral sex or, indeed, marital sex without love.

In some ways, of course, homosexual sex is *less* sinful. The heterosexual who chooses in marriage to use contraception, or who masturbates, is turning away from a viable alternative: a unitive, procreative sexual life. The homosexual has no such option; she is denied, because of something she cannot change, a sexual act which is both unitive and procreative. If a lesbian had sexual relations with a man, she could be procreative but not unitive, because she couldn't fully love him. And if she had sex with another woman, she could be unitive in her emotions but, because of biology, not procreative. So the lesbian is trapped by the Church's teaching, excluded from a loving relationship for no fault of her own; and doomed to a loveless life as a result.

The Church urges compassion for such people (a teaching which, somewhere along the way, seems to have escaped Buchanan). But the Church's real compassion is reserved for another group of people who, like homosexuals, are unable, through no fault of their own, to have unitive and procreative sex: infertile heterosexuals. The Church expresses its compassion not by excluding these couples from the sacrament of marriage, but by including them. Sterile couples are allowed to marry in church and to have sex; so are couples in which the wife is post-menopausal. It's understood that such people have no choice in the matter; they may indeed long to have unitive and procreative sex; and to have children. They are just tragically unable, as the Church sees it, to experience the joy of a procreative married life.

No Good Case Against Gay Marriage

The question, of course, is: Why doesn't this apply to homosexuals? In official teaching, the Church has conceded (Buchanan hedges on this point) that some homosexuals "are definitively such because of some kind of innate instinct or a pathological constitution judged to be incurable." They may want, with all the will in the world, to have a unitive and procreative relationship; they can even intend to be straight. But they can't and they aren't. So why aren't they allowed to express their love as humanely as they possibly can, along with the infertile and the elderly?

The theologians' best answer to this is simply circular. Marriage, they assert, is by definition between a man and a woman. When pressed further, they venture: well, sexual relations between two infertile heterosexuals could, by a miracle, yield a child. But, if it's a miracle you're counting on, why couldn't it happen to two gay people? Who is to put a limit on the power of God? Well, the Church counters, homosexuality isn't natural, it's an "objective disorder." But what is infertility if it isn't a disorder? The truth is, as the current doctrine now stands, the infertile are defined by love and compassion, while homosexuals are defined by loneliness and sin. The Church has no good case why this should be so.

SAME SEX MARRIAGE

Eleanor Mill. Reprinted by permission of Mill NewsArt Syndicate.

I harp on this issue of the infertile for one delicate reason: Patrick and Shelley Buchanan do not have kids. Why not? Generally, I wouldn't dream of bringing up such a question, but I am merely adhering to the same rules Buchanan has laid out for me. From the public absence of his children, as from the public statement of my homosexuality, I can infer certain things about Buchanan's "lifestyle." Either Buchanan is using contraception, in which case he is a hypocrite; or he or his wife is infertile, and he is, one assumes, engaging in non-procreative sex. Either way, I can see no good reason why his sexual life is any more sinful than mine.

THE NEED FOR COMPASSION

Of course, by merely bringing up Buchanan's childlessness, I will be judged to have exceeded the bounds of legitimate debate. But why doesn't the same outrage attach to Buchanan for his fulminations against others whose inability to lead a procreative married life is equally involuntary? Of course, Buchanan goes even further: because of what he infers about my private sexual life, he would celebrate discrimination against me and use the bully pulpit of a campaign to defame me. Why is it unthinkable that someone should apply the same standards to him?

I'll tell you why it's unthinkable. No one should be singled out and stigmatized for something he cannot change, especially if that something is already a source of pain and struggle. Indeed, I would regard anyone's inability to have children, if he wanted to, to be a sadness I should privately sympathize with and publicly say nothing about. Why, I wonder, cannot Buchanan express the same compassion and fairness for me?

> "No same-sex union can realize the
> unique and full potential which the
> marital relationship expresses."

THE ROMAN CATHOLIC CHURCH
CANNOT SANCTION GAY MARRIAGE

Joseph Charron and William Skylstad

In the following viewpoint, Catholic Bishops Joseph Charron and
William Skylstad argue that the Roman Catholic Church cannot
allow homosexuals to marry. They contend that only heterosexual unions can fulfill God's requirement that marriages be both
loving and procreative. Despite its opposition to same-sex
unions, however, the church teaches that homosexuals deserve
compassion, respect, and sympathy, the authors maintain.

As you read, consider the following questions:

1. According to Charron and Skylstad, how does the Roman
   Catholic Church define marriage?
2. In the authors' opinion, why is Christian marriage more than
   a contract?
3. Why do the authors believe that the church's opposition to
   gay marriage is not a form of discrimination?

Reprinted from Joseph Charron and William Skylstad, "Statement on Same-Sex Unions,"
Origins, August 1, 1996, with permission. Copyright 1996 Catholic News Service.

The Roman Catholic Church believes that marriage is a faithful, exclusive and lifelong union between one man and one woman joined as husband and wife in an intimate partnership of life and love. This union was established by God with its own proper laws. By reason of its very nature, therefore, marriage exists for the mutual love and support of the spouses and for the procreation and education of children. These two purposes, the unitive and the procreative, are equal and inseparable. The institution of marriage has a very important relationship to the continuation of the human race, to the total development of the human person and to the dignity, stability, peace and prosperity of the family and of society.

MARRIAGE AS SACRAMENT

Furthermore, we believe the natural institution of marriage has been blessed and elevated by Christ to the dignity of a sacrament. This means that Christian marriage is more than a contract. Because they are married in the Lord, the spouses acquire a special relationship to each other and to society. Their love becomes a living image of the manner in which the Lord personally loves his people and is united with them. Living a Christian, sacramental marriage becomes their fundamental way of attaining salvation.

Hunter. Reprinted by permission of *The Washington Times*.

TRADITIONAL MARRIAGE MUST BE PRESERVED

Because the marital relationship offers benefits unlike any other to persons, to society and to the church, we wish to make it clear that the institution of marriage, as the union of one man and one woman, must be preserved, protected and promoted in both private and public realms. At a time when family life is under significant stress, the principled defense of marriage is an urgent necessity for the well-being of children and families, and for the common good of society.

Thus, we oppose attempts to grant the legal status of marriage to a relationship between persons of the same sex. No same-sex union can realize the unique and full potential which the marital relationship expresses. For this reason, our opposition to "same-sex marriage" is not an instance of unjust discrimination or animosity toward homosexual persons. In fact, the Catholic Church teaches emphatically that individuals and society must respect the basic human dignity of all persons, including those with a homosexual orientation. Homosexual persons have a right to and deserve our respect, compassion, understanding and defense against bigotry, attacks and abuse.

We therefore urge Catholics and all our fellow citizens to commit themselves both to upholding the human dignity of every person and to upholding the distinct and irreplaceable community of marriage.

"The placement of a child in a
homosexual household puts a child
at risk."

HOMOSEXUAL PARENTING IS
HARMFUL TO CHILDREN

Robert H. Knight and Daniel S. Garcia

In the following viewpoint, Robert H. Knight and Daniel S. Garcia argue that homosexual parenting is bad for children. Children
raised by homosexuals live in unstable environments where they
are likely to be harmed by constant exposure to an abnormal
form of human sexuality, the authors maintain. For example, they
contend, research has shown that children growing up in homosexual households experience myriad psychological problems,
including social isolation, difficulties in relationships, confusion
over gender identity, and increased risk of becoming homosexual. To develop normally, children must be raised in traditional
heterosexual families, the authors conclude. Knight is director of
cultural studies at the Family Research Council, a research and
educational organization that promotes the traditional family.
Garcia is a research assistant at the Family Research Council.

As you read, consider the following questions:

1. What flaws are seen in most studies on homosexual
   parenting, according to researchers cited by Knight and
   Garcia?
2. According to Knight and Garcia, what characteristics of the
   homosexual lifestyle reveal that homosexual relationships are
   unstable?

Abridged from Robert H. Knight and Daniel S. Garcia, "Homosexual Parenting: Bad for
Children, Bad for Society," *Family Research Council Insight*, May 1994. Reprinted with
permission. Endnotes in the original have been omitted in this reprint.

S everal recent high-profile cases have put the issue of homosexual adoption on the public agenda. Proponents of homosexual adoption claim that homosexual couples are as capable of
raising children as anyone else. They argue that prohibiting homosexual adoption is unfair discrimination.

However, a closer look at the issue shows that:

- Homosexual adoption is not in the best interest of children.
- Children need both a same-sex and an opposite-sex parent
in order to have the best chance to develop healthy sexual
identities.
- Homosexual households are not a suitable environment for
the development of children because of their instability and
their hostility toward natural families.
- The issue is being driven more by its perceived power to
advance the homosexual agenda than by a concern about
what is best for children.

In deciding who should be allowed to adopt children, the
primary concern for any society must be what is in the best interest of the child. Children should not be placed deliberately in
high-risk situations. Proponents of homosexual adoption often
defend their view as an issue of freedom and individual rights,
putting their political and social agenda ahead of the possible
impact on children. But adopting children is not a right. Children are not commodities to be parceled out. They are individuals with psychological, emotional, social and developmental
needs. And they have the right to expect society to intervene in
parental matters only when a child is at risk. Judging by what
we already know works best for children, the placement of a
child in a homosexual household puts a child at risk.

A LOOK AT THE RESEARCH

Studies on the effects of homosexual parenting on children are
scant, highly politicized, and conducted largely by lesbian researchers in very limited samples. But what research can't tell us
about homosexual parenting, common sense can. We don't need
studies to tell us that it is unwise to let children play unpro-
tected near highways. Likewise, we don't need research to tell us
that it is unwise to have children raised by people with known
sexual and gender identity disorders.

Most studies on homosexual parenting that do exist are seriously flawed. Researcher Frederick W. Bozett, who contends that
children raised by homosexual fathers are no more likely to become homosexual than children raised in normal households,

acknowledges in *Homosexuality and the Family* that:

> Most studies of gay fathers are based on nonrandom small sample sizes, with subjects who are Caucasian, middle- to upper-class, well educated with occupations commensurate with their education, who come mostly from urban centers, and who are relatively accepting of their homosexuality. There is severely limited knowledge of gay fathers who vary from these demographics. Moreover, the validity and reliability of the instruments used in the studies reported are not always addressed.

Other shortcomings of homosexual parenting studies, according to psychologist J. Craig Peery, include: "unsuitable philosophical approaches, logical inconsistencies, inappropriate theoretical models, limitations on sample size, sample selection, control groups, data collection and analysis, and lack of a longitudinal perspective." Psychologist Paul Cameron, who has analyzed the most prominent studies of homosexual households, says that they all have severe shortcomings.

Nonetheless, even within these biased studies, greater risks to children raised in homosexual households are evident, Cameron notes. For starters, most of the studies compare children in homosexual households to those in single-parent households instead of mom-and-dad households. Research shows that children in single-parent households are at higher risk for susceptibility to peer pressure, early sexual activity, drug abuse, delinquency and other problems. Again, not all children raised in single-parent households suffer from such maladies, but they are statistically at a higher risk. So comparing homosexual households with single-parent households is a way to avoid the obvious, documentable desirability of the mom-and-dad household.

INCREASED RISKS FOR CHILDREN

In addition, the studies reveal some examples of elevated risks for children raised in homosexual households. Although activists claim that homosexual households have no discernible impact on sexual identities of the children raised in them, the aggregate data in several studies indicate that children in such households are "about four times more apt to produce homosexual children," according to Dr. Cameron. A close look at the data reveal: *children raised in homosexual households are more likely to become homosexual.*

Data analyzed by Cameron show that 8.9% of children in homosexual households became homosexual while only 2.4% of the children raised in heterosexual households became homosexual.

In a subset of those studies, extracted because they reflect developed, not merely developing, homosexual orientation, Cameron found that 13.9% of children raised in homosexual households became homosexual.

Dr. Jerry Binger, himself a homosexual parent and a co-investigator with Frederick Bozett, writes: "12 percent [of children raised in homosexual households] tend to develop a homosexual orientation."

In a 1989 survey of women once married to men who practice homosexuality, nearly 12% report homosexual behavior in their children. Considering that homosexuals make up less than two percent of the general population, these numbers show a dramatically elevated risk.

Children raised in homosexual households experience emotional problems associated with their parents' homosexuality. The 1989 study of women once married to men who practice homosexuality also showed that one in three mothers with older children report that their children have "problems in relationships with members of the opposite sex."

Another study in *Homosexuality and the Family* showed that 5 out of 9 daughters of divorced lesbians had "felt negatively about their mothers' lesbianism."

Dr. Cameron also found that "58.8% of the children of lesbians and 21.1% of the children of homosexual fathers experience relationship problems with other people because of their knowledge of their parents' homosexuality."

OTHER DANGERS

Other studies by researchers who do not openly promote homosexual adoption find even greater risks to children in homosexual households. In the only random study on homosexual parenting, Dr. Cameron found that children in these households are at far greater risk in a number of areas:

1. *Greater risk of sexual involvement with a parent.* Twenty-nine percent of those raised by at least one homosexual parent reported having had sex with the homosexual parent. Less than one percent (0.6%) of the children of heterosexuals reported having had sex with one of their parents.

2. *Greater risk of becoming homosexual.* Forty-seven percent of those raised by at least one homosexual parent reported a less than exclusively heterosexual orientation.

3. *Greater risk of social or psychological problems.* A disproportionate number of the children reared in homosexual households experienced gender dissatisfaction, and other problems associated with their family environment. These problems included:

- children feeling betrayed by their parents;
- divorce and single parenthood;
- children being orphaned due to short homosexual life span.

According to psychologist Brad Hayton, children from homosexual households:

> . . . fear being labeled a homosexual themselves, fear ostracism from peers, experience much confusion and withdrawal from family and peers. Boys feel left out, girls increasingly worry about their own sexual identity, and many children simply reject their parents' lifestyle. The rotating partners of homosexuals cause many children to compete for the affection of their mothers and feel left out of their own families.

There is a huge body of research showing that children grow up to be much like their parents, according to psychologist J. Craig Peery of Brigham Young University. "Children from large families are more likely to have larger families," Peery says. "Children's educational attainment, career choice, etc. are similar to their parents'. Children who experience their parents' divorce are more likely to become divorced." Children of alcoholics often become alcoholics themselves. Children who suffer child abuse often become child abusers. Children in Roman Catholic families tend to become Roman Catholics. It is reasonable to assume that children raised in homosexual households would be more likely either to become homosexual themselves or to become sexually promiscuous, and the little research available bears this out.

WHAT CHILDREN SEE

Homosexual households are incapable of providing adequate role modeling for several relationships that are crucial to the formation of healthy, stable families. These are the interactions between:
- Husbands and wives
- Mothers and fathers
- Men and women

The mom-and-dad family is the natural environment for child rearing, and is the foundation of civilization. This is reflected in cultures the world over. As noted by the late Harvard sociologist Pitirim Sorokin:

> Marriage is a social evidence of the physical, mental, emotional, spiritual, and civic maturity of the individual. It involves the momentous transformation of a boy into a husband-father, and of a girl into a wife-mother, with corresponding changes in their social position, privileges, and responsibilities.

Sorokin also notes that traditional parenting is the culmination of marriage's meaning for individuals and for society:

Enjoying the marital union in its infinite richness, parents freely fulfill many other paramount tasks. They maintain the procreation of the human race. Through their progeny they determine the hereditary and acquired characteristics of future generations. Through marriage they achieve a social immortality of their own, of their ancestors, and of their particular groups and community. This immortality is secured through the transmission of their name and values, and of their traditions and ways of life to their children, grandchildren, and later generations.

Despite all of the new technology of contraception, it takes two opposite sex people to create children. It takes two opposite sex people to nurture and raise children properly until they can care for themselves. In terms of sexual development: Boys need fathers so they can develop their own sexual identity; they need mothers so they can learn how to interact with the opposite sex. Girls need mothers so they can learn what it is to be a woman; they need fathers so they know how to interact with the opposite sex.

CHILDREN NEED HETEROSEXUAL PARENTS

How many lives will be broken, how many little experiments will suffer in silence (unobserved by omniscient researchers) before courts and social scientists learn you can't fool nature? Children were meant to be nurtured by a man and woman together. Absent that, at least they shouldn't be placed in a situation where a distorted version of human sexuality is presented as the norm, to satisfy the latest bizarre demands for equality.

Don Feder, *Human Events*, October 16, 1993.

In single-parent families, children are already at a disadvantage in terms of viewing the crucial relationships between the sexes; in homosexual households they are at far greater risk because not only is one of the sexes absent but the children view aberrant sexuality on a daily basis. Their understanding of sexuality is seriously distorted through the homosexual lens, as is attested by some who have grown up in homosexual households and are now speaking out.

For example, Jakii Edwards said of her upbringing in a lesbian household: "I had to 'prove' my femininity, and I did that by becoming promiscuous with men." She also observed that this is a common reaction among children raised in lesbian households. "Many of these children overcompensate in an effort to prove that they are not like their parents." After many hours of therapeutic counseling, she emerged with a healthy sexual identity and is now counseling others who were raised in homosexual households.

Edwards says that lesbians can be loving care-givers but she notes that "it does not matter how loving and kind lesbian parents are. These households can't teach proper interactions." She warns of anger, gender confusion and self-esteem problems, along with embarrassment and shame, among children raised in lesbian households. Also, the "normal adolescent rebellion is magnified and resentment and tension increase in lesbian households."

GENDER IDENTITY

Dr. Elizabeth Moberly, a psychologist who specializes in gender identity research, says homosexual behavior is an unconscious effort on the part of homosexuals to recover their natural sexual identity. In her ground-breaking 1979 book *Psychogenesis*, Moberly describes how homosexuality stems from an unmet psychological need:

> The repressed love-need of the young child may be reactivated in later years. This is the phenomenon which, when it happens to involve a love-source of the same sex, is labelled homosexual. On our data, this condition is essentially the reactivation of a thwarted infantile love-need, that has persisted unmet and hence still requires to be met. We are not, however, suggesting on account of this that homosexuality is not truly involved in this condition. What we are suggesting is that this is the so-called homosexual condition in its essence, viz. an unmet need for love from the parent of the same sex.

She goes on to explain that homosexuals experience ambivalence when they have same-sex relations because the behavior is the erotic embodiment of the emotional need to bond with the same sex rather than a rejection of the opposite sex:

> Homosexuality . . . is fundamentally a problem of gender identity, rather than of sexuality as such. . . . The homosexual's love for men is but the boy's thwarted love for his father, i.e. it is a masculine and an identificatory love which is intimately linked with the building of the boy's gender identity. Hence it is in no way analogous to the love of the female for the male, since this latter kind of love does not aim at fulfilling an incomplete gender identity, but rather presupposes the completion of the identificatory process.

Since homosexual love is quite different from the love a wife gives to her husband, a wife cannot simply be replaced by a male partner without a monumental change in the entire psychology of the household. It is unreasonable to assume that the sexuality of the partners makes no difference, and that children in a homosexual household will see, hear and experience what they would in a husband-wife household. . . .

INSTABILITY IS A FACTOR

The homosexual lifestyle is inconsistent with the proper raising of children. Because homosexual relationships are characteristically unstable, they are less likely to provide children the security they need. While there are some homosexuals who have stable, monogamous relationships and live what appear to be relatively normal lives, most:

- *Show a high degree of promiscuity.* The average male homosexual has 50 sex partners each year. One study found that 43 percent of white male homosexuals estimated that they had sex with 500 or more partners, and 28 percent with 1,000 or more. Only 2 percent of homosexuals could be considered monogamous;
- *Have an unhealthy attitude toward the opposite sex.* Lesbian culture is rife with anti-male sentiment, as evidenced by hostility toward men in lesbian publications and in public references. Even if two lesbians work hard to conceal their own bitterness toward men, their social milieu consists of people who are largely hostile to men, the very people that a boy needs to observe to develop a secure gender identity. Likewise, a homosexual male household is missing a proper appreciation of the feminine, ignoring it or identifying with exaggerated portrayals of "vamp" femininity such as Madonna;
- *Have fleeting relationships.* The average male homosexual live-in relationship lasts between two and three years. Before living together, 64 percent of homosexuals knew each other for less than a year. A mere 26 percent believe that commitment is most important in a marriage relationship;
- *Experience extracurricular relationships,* even in so-called "monogamous" relationships. Former homosexual William Aaron explains:

In the gay life, fidelity is almost impossible. Since part of the compulsion of homosexuality seems to be a need on the part of the homophile to 'absorb' masculinity from his sexual partners, he must be constantly on the lookout for [new partners]. Constantly the most successful homophile 'marriages' are those where there is an arrangement between the two to have affairs on the side while maintaining the semblance of permanence in their living arrangement.

On the issue of homosexual "marriage," Dr. Brad Hayton writes: "Homosexuals . . . model a poor view of marriage to children. They [children] are taught by example and belief that marital relationships are transitory and mostly sexual in nature. Sexual relationships are primarily for pleasure rather than procreation. And they [children] are taught that monogamy in a marriage is not the norm [and] should be discouraged if one wants a good 'marital' relationship."

Apart from the heightened possibility of the child in a homosexual household being exposed to parents' outside partners, homosexual sex practices are especially unhealthy. Homosexuals account for a disproportionate number of the most serious sexually transmitted diseases, including AIDS, syphilis, gonorrhea, genital warts, Hepatitis A, Hepatitis B, and tuberculosis. Homosexuals typically have shorter life expectancy. They are also more likely to display risky, self-destructive behavior such as alcoholism and drug abuse. . . .

THE BEDROCK OF SOCIETY

The mom-and-dad family has long been recognized as the bedrock of civil society around the world. No institution is more important in shaping children than the family. Children need and deserve the best environment possible in which to learn and grow. The traditional mom-and-dad family provides this, while homosexual relationships do not. Homosexual relationships are not the equivalent of marriage, and children should not be placed into homosexual households.

> "Gay and lesbian people can be
> equally as good at parenting as
> heterosexuals."

HOMOSEXUAL PARENTING IS NOT HARMFUL TO CHILDREN

Gary Sanders

Families headed by gays and lesbians are as healthy as families headed by heterosexuals, contends Gary Sanders in the following viewpoint. No reliable evidence has shown that a parent's homosexuality affects a child's psychological health, social adjustment, or sexual orientation, he maintains. Moreover, Sanders argues, the contention that gay and lesbian parenting damages children is based on homophobic and unsubstantiated beliefs about homosexuality that are often promoted by right-wing, antigay advocacy organizations. Sanders is the associate director of the Family Therapy Program and director of the Human Sexuality Program at the Faculty of Medicine at the University of Calgary in Canada.

As you read, consider the following questions:
1. According to Sanders, when was the term "homosexual" first coined?
2. What is the American Pediatric Association's position on homosexuality, according to the author?
3. According to Sanders, why is Paul Cameron an unreliable source of information for research on gay and lesbian parenting?

Reprinted from Gary Sanders, "Normal Families: Research on Gay and Lesbian Parenting." This article first appeared in the January 1998 issue of *In the Family* and is used here with permission of the publisher. Copyright In the Family. For back issues or subscription information call 301-270-4771.

Recently, the newspapers in Edmonton, Alberta, were filled with the story of the refusal of the Provincial Child Welfare System to allow a woman, who had been a highly regarded foster mother to more than 70 children, to receive further foster child placements when it was discovered that she was in a lesbian relationship. The government officials stated that only traditional, "normal" families were appropriate as foster parents. The officials defined "normal" as "a family with a mother and a father."

One of the great myths about families is that gay and lesbian people do not have children or families, either by reproduction or by adoption. The designation "normal family" has historically been co-opted by a heterosexual married union with offspring. However, M.A. Gold and colleagues, in the 1994 article "Children of Gay or Lesbian Parents" in *Pediatrics in Review*, point out that in the United States, fewer than one third of children live in a so-called traditional family, with a working father, homemaking mother and one or more children. Therefore, the understanding of "normal" family has grown to include single-parent families, families that are blended (i.e., remarried with children), and families that are led by one or two parents who are lesbian- or gay-identified. Despite the enlargement of the notion of family to include this diversity, the right-wing often speaks of a "threat to family values" by gay and lesbian parents, despite lack of research support.

Myths About Homosexuality

Dr. Lorne Warneke of the University of Alberta has written extensively on this issue, including a 1997 amicus brief entitled "When Virtually Normal is Normal Enough: Homosexual Orientation and Parenting." He outlines four myths that are used to support a prejudicial and unfounded position against gay and lesbian people being effective parents. It is useful to examine those myths and then the research on gay and lesbian parenting that addresses each one.

• Myth #1: *Homosexuality is only a chosen lifestyle.* Common sense suggests that an individual does not choose a homosexual orientation, because it is unlikely anyone would consciously choose to be vilified and denigrated by centuries of persecution. Some women and men have chosen to be lesbian and gay for various reasons, but the majority of homosexuals don't choose to have homosexual attractions; it is simply a fact of their existence. Research on gay men shows that sexual orientation occurs long before conscious choice is even available for an individual's action and/or awareness. Recent research is indicating that homosexuality has a degree of biologic predetermination. However, whether it is biologically predetermined or culturally instilled through as yet too complicated processes of early development, what is known is that one's affiliative sexual orientation is indelible, just as one's concept of self as male or female is indelible.

There is a significant amount of research data to support claims of a biological basis for male homosexuality. For example, writer Chandler Burr's 1996 book, *A Separate Creation*, goes into great depth on the question of research regarding the existence of a "gay gene" described by Dean Hamer and colleagues in a 1993 *Science* article, "A Linkage Between DNA Markers on the X Chromosome and Male Sexual Orientation." The hypothesis that there is a "gay gene" was also explored by Simon LeVay in his book *The Sexual Brain*, and in his article, "The Evidence of Biological Influence on Male Homosexuality," published in *Scientific American* in 1994. Even before LeVay and Hamer came out with their findings, others such as D. Swaab and M. Hofman had published research on biological differences between heterosexual and gay men in a 1990 issue of the journal *Brain Research*. (Research on lesbians has not been done because systemic sexism minimizes research on women.)

GAYNESS IS NORMAL

• *Myth 2: Gay and lesbian people are psychologically maladjusted.* The concept of homosexual orientation, as well as the concept of heterosexuality, is a fairly recent creation, according to historian Jonathan Katz in his book *The Invention of Heterosexuality*. It was a German lawyer, Karl Heinrich Ulrichs, who published a series of booklets in 1864, who first coined the term homosexual. The term was incorporated into the English vocabulary just before the turn of the century. Ulrichs suggested that homosexuals are normal people, that homosexuality is inborn, and that sexual relationships between members of the same sex are based on love. He went on to argue that homosexuals should have the right to marry one another. Magnus Hirshfeld, a famous early-twentieth-century German sexologist, also believed that homosexuality was inborn and a normal of variant sexual expression. However, it was Sigmund Freud, in his famous "Letter to an American Mother" of a gay son, who spoke to the inherent normality of gayness and published the first widespread professional disagreement with the myth of homosexuality as pathological. The Kinsey reports of 1948 and 1949 on the sexual behavior of men and women showed that homosexuality was omnipresent, although at one-tenth the rate of heterosexuality. Yet it was the classic studies by Evelyn Hooker that demonstrated that homosexuals and heterosexuals could not be differentiated by a battery of psychological personality tests when read blind by trained professionals. In other words, individuals with a homosexual orientation were as normal in terms of psychological makeup and emotional maturity as heterosexuals. Other studies have been done to reaffirm her findings of normal psychological development and the fact that there is no higher incidence of mental illness in gay or lesbian persons compared to heterosexuals. Some of those include M. Weinberg and C. Williams's 1974 work, *Male Homosexuals: Their Problems and Adaptations*, a 1971 article in the *Journal of Abnormal Psychology* by N. Thompson and colleagues entitled "Personal Adjustment of Male and Female Homosexuals and Heterosexuals," an even earlier study—1969—in the *British Journal of Psychiatry* by J. Hopkins called "The Lesbian Personality" and others.

Once the major professional organizations of the mental health field declassified homosexuality as a mental disorder, a process that began back in 1973 with the American Psychiatric Association, the official consensus in the field has been that homosexuality should not be seen as a condition that necessitates change, "conversion" or any pathologizing. In fact, the American Pediatric Association stated that trying to change gay or lesbian sexual orientation would be unethical and grounds for malpractice. Therefore, the idea that gay and lesbian people are somehow less mentally healthy, well-adjusted, or able to cope compared to their heterosexual brothers and sisters can be put to rest for good. Of course, as with any group, some persons who are gay and lesbian may have psychiatric or psychological disorders, but this occurs no more or less often than in the rest of the population.

WHAT THE RESEARCH SAYS

• Myth #3: *Gay and lesbian people cannot be good parents.* This myth is often touted by those with homophobic and heterosexist agendas; however, not only does the research refute this belief, it also points out that, in fact, gay and lesbian people can be equally as good at parenting as heterosexuals. Seldom in the area of psychological, sociological, anthropological, psychiatric, and medical research has there been such agreement amongst researchers as there is on this issue.

There has been considerable research done in the area of parenting abilities of gays and lesbians, the effects on children of being raised by gays and lesbians and studies comparing heterosexual parents with lesbian and gay parents. M. Kirkpatrick has shown in an article in the *Journal of Homosexuality*, "Clinical Implications of Lesbian Mother Studies," that findings from studies comparing lesbian and heterosexual mothers show no difference with respect to maternal attitude. In a 1981 article in the *American Journal of Orthopsychiatry*, "Children's Acquisition of Sex-Role Behavior in Lesbian Mother Families," B. Hoeffer indicated that lesbian and heterosexual mothers are very similar with respect to childrearing and maternal interest. Fiona Tasker and colleagues conducted a longitudinal study of 25 young adults from lesbian families compared to 21 young adults raised by heterosexual single mothers and, as their 1991 *Family Law* article revealed, they discovered that the former compared to the latter as well-adjusted psychologically, both in terms of well-being and of family identity and relationships. Lesbian mothers on average are found to be as child-oriented, warm and responsive, nurturing and confident with their children as were their heterosexual counterparts. Lesbians may even do a better job in some cases— there have been findings that show that lesbian mothers after divorce are more likely to ensure their children have male role models compared to heterosexual mothers.

Successful Families

Lesbian and gay parents are not a new phenomenon. There are an estimated 5 million to 6 million of them in this country, most of whom became parents in the context of a heterosexual marriage before they were fully aware of their sexual orientation. What is new, however, is that since the 1970s lesbians and gay men, perhaps tens of thousands, are choosing to become parents through adoption and artificial insemination. As the stigma evaporates and visibility increases, word is getting around among adoption, health care and child welfare professionals that families headed by lesbians and gays are working out successfully.

April Martin, *Insight*, July 25, 1994.

As for gay fathers, F.W. Bozett compared parenting between gay and heterosexual fathers in a 1989 review of the literature in the *Journal of Homosexuality*, and found no differences between the two groups in terms of problem-solving and providing recreation for their children. Gay fathers were found to be less traditional, demonstrated greater nurturing, had more investment in the parental role, and were more positive about this, than heterosexual fathers. These findings have been backed up by several research studies by J. Bigner and R. Jacobsen. Charlotte Patterson, in her comprehensive review of the subject of children raised by gays or lesbians ("Children of Lesbians and Gays," in a 1992 issue of *Child Development*) writes, "There is no evidence to suggest the psychosocial development among children of gay men or lesbians is compromised in any respect relative to that among offspring of heterosexual parents." She goes on to say, "Indeed, the evidence to date suggest that home environment provided by gay and lesbian parents are as likely as those provided by heterosexual parents to support and enable children's psychosocial growth." Bigner and Jacobsen conclude, "There is no evidence that being gay is a liability as far as parenting is concerned"; and "it appears that gay fathers are at least equal to heterosexual fathers in the quality of their parenting."

While there is a long bibliography of research that upholds the idea that lesbians and gays can make fine parents, there is no evidence to suggest that gays and lesbians are less capable than heterosexuals with respect to parenting skills and attitudes. There has only been one researcher, Paul Cameron, who has repeatedly spoken, written, and published on this point; however, he was discredited by his own professional associations as having fabricated his research on gay and lesbian parenting to fit with his preconceived homophobic belief system. Despite his being dismissed from his professional association and discredited by his scientific peers, there are those with an agenda of intolerance and prejudice who continue to cite his writings as if they had credence.

HOMOPHOBIC WORRIES

Two additional fears are often raised by those who are opposed to gay and lesbian parenting: One is that there may be a higher preponderance of gay and lesbian children because their parents are openly lesbian and gay. Despite the inherent heterosexist and homophobic premise that more lesbian or gay children would be undesirable, the concern is not supported in any research. For instance, researcher R. Green, in his 1978 article in the *American Journal of Psychiatry*, "Sexual Identity of 37 Children Raised By Homosexual or Transsexual Parents," and J.M. Bailey and colleagues, in their 1995 article in *Developmental Psychology*, "Sexual Orientation of Adult Sons of Gay Fathers," and—most recently—S. Golombok and F. Task, in the 1996 article in *Developmental Psychology*, "Do Parents Influence the Sexual Orientation of Their Children: Findings from a Longitudinal Study of Lesbian Families," showed the incidence of homosexuality in offspring of gay and lesbian people, or those raised by gay and lesbian people, as being no different than in the general population.

A second worry is that children raised by gay and lesbian parents will show emotional or social maladjustment because of stigmatization. This is based on the assumption that children of homosexual parents may be more likely to experience social trauma due to stigmatization, social isolation, parental divorce, and being raised in a single-parent household. All the studies found that the children of gay fathers or lesbian mothers have normal peer relationships, develop close friendships and do not suffer adversely from stigmatization because of having a parent who happens to be homosexual. We must certainly expect that the children of gay parents will have to cope with prejudice, misunderstanding, and possibly even negative peer reactions. But then, so may the children of African American parents, poor Appalachian parents, divorced parents, and parents with physical impairments. The fact that a child's parents are different from the majority of white, middle-class, unimpaired parents is not usually considered an appropriate reason for removing a child from a home. Therefore, sexual preference should not be any different in this respect.

TWO MISTAKEN BELIEFS

• *Myth #4: Children of gay or lesbian parents are at greater risk for sexual abuse.* This myth can easily be jettisoned since no research whatsoever supports it. It seems that the myth is perpetuated by two mistaken beliefs: first, that there is a higher incidence of pedophilia amongst gay men than in the heterosexual population, and secondly, that therefore gay fathers are more likely to abuse their sons.

As regards the incidence of pedophilia, interestingly, there appears to be proportionally fewer homosexual pedophiles than heterosexual pedophiles. Three key studies bear this out: C. Jenny and colleagues' 1994 article in *Pediatrics,* "Are Children at Risk for Abuse By Homosexuals?"; D.E. Newton's 1978 article in *Adolescence,* "Homosexual Behavior and Child Molestation: A Review of the Evidence"; and A. Groth and H.J. Birnbaum's 1978 study in *Arch Sexual Behaviors,* "Adult Sexual Orientation and Attraction to Underage Persons." Additionally, the research indicates that sexual molestation of children is essentially a heterosexual act with familial incest almost always being father-daughter in type. Even in those situations where a boy is sexually interfered with by a father, the father is disproportionally self-identified as heterosexual.

Warneke sums up the relevant recent literature on the issue of gay and lesbian parenting by saying: "With almost boring repetition, the conclusions of all the major studies, reviews and opinions of experts in the field were virtually the same. All of this is best summarized by B. Maddox in a classic article where she stated, 'What does sexual preference have to do with the need to love and care for children? Not much, according to studies and interviews with married and divorced homosexuals.'"

PERIODICAL BIBLIOGRAPHY

The following articles have been selected to supplement the diverse views presented in this chapter. Addresses are provided for periodicals not indexed in the *Readers' Guide to Periodical Literature*, the *Alternative Press Index*, the *Social Sciences Index*, or the *Index to Legal Periodicals and Books*.

Julie Brienza	"Same-Sex Marriage: Equal Rights or Death of Family?" *Trial*, December 1996.
Frank Bruni	"A Small-but-Growing Sorority Is Giving Birth to Children for Gay Men," *NewYork Times*, June 25, 1998.
Michael Colberg	"With Open Arms: The Emotional Journey of Gay and Lesbian Adoption," *In the Family*, July 1996. Available from PO Box 5387, Takoma Park, MD 20913.
David Orgon Coolidge	"Same-Sex Marriage: As Hawaii Goes," *First Things*, April 1997. Available from the Institute on Religion and Public Life, 156 Fifth Ave., Suite 400, New York, NY 10010.
Dwight Daniels	"Let's Invite Gay and Lesbian Catholics to a Church Wedding," *U.S. Catholic*, November 1997.
Randy Dotinga	"Holy Matrimony," *Advocate*, April 14, 1998.
William N. Eskridge and Bob Barr	"Would Legal Recognition of Same-Sex Marriage Be Good for America?" *Insight*, June 10, 1996. Available from 3600 NewYork Ave. NE, Washington, DC 20002.
David Frum	"The Courts, Gay Marriage, and the Popular Will," *Weekly Standard*, September 30, 1996. Available from New America Publishing, Inc., 1211 Avenue of the Americas, NewYork, NY 10036.
Jeffrey G. Gibson	"To Love, Honor, and Build a Life: A Case for Same-Gender Marriage," *Human Rights*, Summer 1996. Available from the ABA Press for the Section of Individual Rights and Responsibilities of the American Bar Association, 750 N. Lake Shore Dr., Chicago, IL 60611.
Kim A. Lawton	"State Lawmakers Scramble to Ban Same-Sex Marriage," *Christianity Today*, February 3, 1997.

William J. Levada   "The San Francisco Solution," *First Things*, August/September 1997.

Martin E. Marty   "Hard Texts, the Whole Gospel," *Christian Century*, October 29, 1997.

Robert Tyminski   "Straight in a Queer World," *In the Family*, January 1997.

FOR FURTHER DISCUSSION

CHAPTER 1

1. Steve Kangas argues that homosexuality is an inherited condition; Steve Calverley and Rob Goetze maintain that there are no solid data linking homosexuality to genetics. What evidence does each author present to support his conclusion? Which viewpoint is more persuasive? Why?

2. Richard Pillard claims that same-sex orientation is most likely rooted in genetics. Cal Thomas and the Illinois Family Institute contend that homosexuality is caused by environmental factors such as traumatic childhood experiences. Charles Lopresto argues that homosexuality is probably the result of a combination of biological and environmental factors. In your opinion, which of these authors presents the strongest case? Explain your answer, using examples from the viewpoints.

3. Erin Blades insists that the causes of homosexuality are unimportant and irrelevant. Simon LeVay maintains that discovering the basis of sexual orientation could increase society's acceptance of gays and lesbians. On what points do these two authors agree? On what points do they disagree?

CHAPTER 2

1. Frances Snowder contends that societal homophobia increases the suicide risk for gay teens. Philip Jenkins argues that activists' reliance on skewed statistics on the percentage of homosexuals in the population has caused many researchers to exaggerate the risk of gay teen suicide. Do you agree with Jenkins that gay rights advocates have "abused rhetoric" to promote their social and political agenda? Why or why not?

2. The viewpoints in this chapter include debate about the claim that homosexuals constitute a minority group and arguments about the passage of antidiscrimination laws for gays and lesbians. After reading this chapter, are you more or less likely to support laws that bar discrimination against gay people? Explain your answer, using evidence from the viewpoints.

CHAPTER 3

1. Rayford Kytle discusses his own experience of coming to terms with a homosexual orientation as part of his argument that society should encourage increased acceptance of homosexuality. The Ramsey Colloquium reviews aspects of traditional Judeo-Christian morality to support their contention that society should not support efforts to legitimize homosex-

ual behavior. Which author's rhetorical technique do you find more compelling? Why?

2. Alice Ogden Bellis and D. James Kennedy disagree about the need for Christians to accept homosexuality. Both authors cite and interpret passages from the Bible as support for their arguments. Compare the discussion of biblical passages in Bellis's viewpoint with that in Kennedy's viewpoint. In your opinion, which author uses his or her analysis of Scripture to better effect?

3. Shelly Reese argues that schools should adopt educational programs that emphasize respect for gays and lesbians, while Ed Vitagliano contends that such programs are inappropriate because they coerce students into supporting the pro-homosexual agenda. Do you believe that educational institutions should openly advocate acceptance of homosexuality? Why or why not? Support your answer with evidence from the viewpoints.

4. The National Association for Research and Therapy of Homosexuality (NARTH) maintains that psychologists must not turn their back on homosexuals who need and want therapy to change their sexual orientation. How do you think the American Psychological Association (APA) would respond to this pronouncement of NARTH's? Explain.

CHAPTER 4

1. Ralph Wedgwood contends that same-sex couples should have the right to marry; Burman Skrable maintains that homosexual marriage would harm society. Compare their opinions, then formulate your own argument about the viability of same-sex marriage in American society.

2. Andrew Sullivan argues that the Roman Catholic Church has no good reason to deny the sacrament of marriage to same-sex couples. What examples does he use to support his argument? Do Joseph Charron, William Skylstad, and Joseph Sobran effectively refute Sullivan's contentions? Why or why not?

3. Robert H. Knight and Daniel S. Garcia maintain that children raised by homosexuals are likely to grow up psychologically and socially maladjusted. Gary Sanders argues that a parent's homosexuality has no effect on a child's emotional health or social adjustment. Which of these authors do you agree with, and why? Support your answer with evidence from the viewpoints.

ORGANIZATIONS TO CONTACT

The editors have compiled the following list of organizations concerned with the issues debated in this book. The descriptions are derived from materials provided by the organizations. All have publications or information available for interested readers. The list was compiled on the date of publication of the present volume; the information provided here may change. Be aware that many organizations take several weeks or longer to respond to inquiries, so allow as much time as possible.

American Civil Liberties Union (ACLU)
Lesbian and Gay Rights/AIDS Project
132 W. 43rd St., New York, NY 10036
(212) 944-9800 • fax: (212) 869-9065
website: http://www.aclu.org

The ACLU is the nation's oldest and largest civil liberties organization. Its Lesbian and Gay Rights/AIDS Project, started in 1986, handles litigation, education, and public-policy work on behalf of gays and lesbians. The union supports same-sex marriage. It publishes the monthly newsletter *Civil Liberties Alert*, the handbook *The Rights of Lesbians and Gay Men*, the briefing paper "Lesbian and Gay Rights," and the book *The Rights of Families: The ACLU Guide to the Rights of Today's Family Members*.

Coalition for Positive Sexuality (CPS)
3712 N. Broadway, Box 191, Chicago, IL 60613
(773) 604-1654
website: http://www.positive.org

CPS is a grassroots direct-action group formed in 1992 by high-school students and activists. It endeavors to counteract the institutionalized misogyny, heterosexism, homophobia, racism, and ageism that students experience at school. It is dedicated to offering teens sex education that is pro-woman, pro-lesbian/gay/bisexual, pro-safe sex, and pro-choice. Numerous pamphlets and publications are available upon request.

Concerned Women for America (CWA)
1015 15th St. NW, Suite 1100, Washington, DC 20005
(202) 488-7000 • fax: (202) 488-0806
website: http://www.cwfa.org

CWA works to strengthen the traditional family according to Judeo-Christian moral standards. It opposes gay marriage and the granting of additional civil rights protections to gays and lesbians. It publishes numerous brochures and policy papers as well as *Family Voice*, a monthly newsmagazine.

Courage
c/o Church of St. John the Baptist
210 W. 31st St., New York, NY 10001
(212) 268-1010 • fax: (212) 268-7150
e-mail: NYCourage@aol.com • website: http://world.std.com/~courage

Courage is a network of spiritual support groups for gay and lesbian Catholics who wish to lead celibate lives in accordance with Roman Catholic teachings on homosexuality. It publishes listings of local groups, a newsletter, and an annotated bibliography of books on homosexuality.

Dignity/USA
1500 Massachusetts Ave. NW, Suite 11, Washington, DC 20005
(800) 877-8797 • (202) 861-0017 • fax: (202) 429-9808
e-mail: dignity@aol.com • website: http://www.dignityusa.org

Dignity/USA is a Roman Catholic organization of gays, lesbians, bisexuals, and their families and friends. It believes that homosexuals and bisexuals can lead sexually active lives in a manner consonant with Christ's teachings. Through its national and local chapters, Dignity/USA provides educational materials, AIDS crisis assistance, and spiritual support groups for members. It publishes the monthly *Dignity Journal* and a book, *Theological/Pastoral Resources: A Collection of Articles on Homosexuality from a Catholic Perspective.*

Exodus International
PO Box 77652, Seattle, WA 98177
(206) 784-7799
website: http://exodus.base.org

Exodus International is a referral network offering support to homosexual Christians desiring to become heterosexual. It publishes the monthly newsletter *Update,* lists of local ministries and programs, and bibliographies of books and tapes on homosexuality.

Family Research Council
801 G St. NW, Washington, DC 20001
(202) 393-2100 • fax: (202) 393-2134
website: http://www.frc.org

The council is a research and educational organization that promotes the traditional family, which the council defines as a group of people bound by marriage, blood, or adoption. The council opposes gay marriage and adoption rights. It publishes numerous reports from a conservative perspective on issues affecting the family, including *Free to Be Family.* Among its publications are the monthly newsletter *Washington Watch* and the bimonthly journal *Family Policy.*

Lambda Legal Defense and Education Fund
120 Wall St., Suite 1500, New York, NY 10005
(212) 809-8585 • fax: (212) 809-0055
website: http://www.lambdalegal.org

Lambda is a public-interest law firm committed to achieving full recognition of the civil rights of lesbians, gay men, and people with HIV/AIDS. The firm addresses a variety of topics, including equal marriage rights, parenting and relationship issues, and domestic-partner benefits. It publishes the quarterly *Lambda Update* as well as numerous pamphlets and position papers.

Love in Action
PO Box 753307, Memphis, TN 38175-3307
(901) 542-3307 • fax: (901) 542-9742
website: http://www.loveinaction.org

Love in Action is a Christian ministry believes that homosexuality is a learned behavior and that all homosexual conduct is wrong because it violates God's laws. It provides support to gays and lesbians to help them convert to heterosexuality. It also offers a residential twelve-step recovery program for individuals who have made the commitment to follow Christ and wish to leave their homosexuality behind. Current publications include a monthly newsletter.

National Association for the Research and Therapy of Homosexuality (NARTH)
16633 Ventura Blvd., Suite 1340, Encino, CA 91436-1801
(818) 789-4440 • fax: (805) 373-5084
website: http://www.narth.com

NARTH is an information and referral network that believes the causes of homosexuality are primarily developmental and that it is usually responsive to psychotherapy. The association supports homosexual men and women who feel that homosexuality is contrary to their value systems and who voluntarily seek treatment. NARTH publishes the *NARTH Bulletin*, the book *Healing Homosexuality: Case Stories of Reparative Therapy*, and numerous conference papers and research articles.

National Center for Lesbian Rights
870 Market St., Suite 570, San Francisco, CA 94102
(415) 392-6257 • fax: (415) 392-8442
e-mail: info@NCLRights.org • website: http://www.nclrights.org

Founded in 1977, the center is an advocacy organization that provides legal counseling and representation for victims of sexual-orientation discrimination. Primary areas of advice include custody and parenting, employment, housing, the military, and insurance. The center publishes the handbooks *Recognizing Lesbian and Gay Families: Strategies for Obtaining Domestic Partners Benefits* and *Lesbian and Gay Parenting: A Psychological and Legal Perspective* as well as other materials.

Parents, Families, and Friends of Lesbians and Gays (PFLAG)
1101 14th St. NW, Suite 1030, Washington, DC 20005
(202) 638-4200 • fax: (202) 638-0243
e-mail: info@pflag.org • website: http://www.pflag.org

PFLAG is a national organization that provides support and educational services for gays, lesbians, bisexuals, and their families and friends. It works to end prejudice and discrimination against homosexual and bisexual persons. It publishes and distributes booklets and papers, including "About Our Children," "Coming Out to My Parents," and "Why Is My Child Gay?"

Reconciling Congregation Program (RCP)
3801 N. Keeler Ave., Chicago, IL 60641
(773) 736-5526 • fax: (773) 736-5475
website: http://www.rcp.org

RCP is a network of United Methodist churches, ministries, and individuals that welcomes and supports lesbians and gay men and seeks to end homophobia and prejudice in the church and society. Its national headquarters provide resources to help local ministries achieve these goals. Among its publications are the quarterly magazine *Open Hands*, the book *And God Loves Each One*, as well as other pamphlets, studies, and videos.

Sex Information and Education Council of the U.S. (SIECUS)
130 W. 42nd St., Suite 2500, New York, NY 10036-7901
(212) 819-9770 • fax: (212) 819-9776

SIECUS is an organization of educators, physicians, social workers, and others who support the individual's right to acquire knowledge about sexuality and who encourage responsible sexual behavior. The council promotes comprehensive sex education for all children that includes AIDS education, teaching about homosexuality, and instruction about contraceptives and sexually transmitted diseases. Its publications include fact sheets, annotated bibliographies by topic, the booklet *Talk About Sex*, and the bimonthly *SIECUS Report*.

Universal Fellowship of Metropolitan Community Churches (UFMCC)
8704 Santa Monica Blvd., 2nd Fl., West Hollywood, CA 90069
(310) 360-8640 • fax: (310) 360-8680
e-mail: info@ufmcchq.com • website: http://www.ufmcc.com

UFMCC works to confront poverty, sexism, racism, and homophobia through Christian social action. Composed of more than three hundred congregations, the fellowship accepts gays, lesbians, and bisexuals and works to incorporate them into the Christian church. UFMCC publications include the quarterly newsletter *Journey*, the brochures *Homosexuality: Not a Sin, Not a Sickness* and *Homosexuality: The Bible as Your Friend*, and the pamphlet *Homosexuality and the Conservative Christian*.

BIBLIOGRAPHY OF BOOKS

Barry D. Adam	*The Rise of a Gay and Lesbian Movement.* New York: Twayne, 1995.
Robert M. Baird and M. Katherine Baird, eds.	*Homosexuality: Debating the Issues.* Amherst, NY: Prometheus Books, 1995.
Robert M. Baird and Stuart E. Rosenbaum, eds.	*Same-Sex Marriage: The Moral and Legal Debate.* Amherst, NY: Prometheus Books, 1997.
Ellen Bass and Kate Kaufman	*Free Your Mind: The Book for Gay, Lesbian, and Bisexual Youth and Their Allies.* New York: HarperPerennial, 1996.
Bruce Bawer, ed.	*Beyond Queer: Challenging Gay Left Orthodoxy.* New York: Free Press, 1996.
Dangerous Bedfellows, ed.	*Queer Politics and the Future of AIDS Activism.* Cambridge, MA: South End Press, 1997.
Mario Bergner	*Setting Love in Order: Hope and Healing for the Homosexual.* Grand Rapids, MI: Baker Book House, 1995.
Robert L. Brawley, ed.	*Biblical Ethics and Homosexuality: Listening to Scripture.* Louisville, KY: Westminster John Knox, 1996.
Larry Dane Brimner	*Being Different: Lambda Youths Speak Out.* Danbury, CT: Franklin Watts, 1996.
Reuven P. Bulka	*One Man, One Woman, One Lifetime: An Argument for Moral Tradition.* Lafayette, LA: Huntington House, 1995.
Jan Clausen	*Beyond Gay or Straight: Understanding Sexual Orientation.* Broomall, PA: Chelsea House, 1996.
D. Merilee Clunis and G. Dorsey Green	*The Lesbian Parenting Book: A Guide to Creating Families and Raising Children.* Seattle: Seal Press, 1995.
William Dannemeyer	*Shadow in the Land: Homosexuality in America.* San Francisco: Ignatius Press, 1995.
Bob Davies and Lori Rentzel	*Coming Out of Homosexuality: New Freedom for Men and Women.* Downers Grove, IL: Intervarsity Press, 1994.
David Deitcher, ed.	*The Question of Equality: Lesbian and Gay Politics Since Stonewall.* New York: Scribner, 1995.
William N. Eskridge	*The Case for Same-Sex Marriage: From Sexual Liberty to Civilized Commitment.* New York: Free Press, 1996.
David M. Estlund and Martha Craven Nussbaum, eds.	*Sex, Preference, and Family: Essays on Laws and Nature.* New York: Oxford University Press, 1996.
Beth Firestein, ed.	*Bisexuality: The Psychology and Politics of an Invisible Minority.* Thousand Oaks, CA: Sage, 1997.

George Grant and Mark A. Horne	*Legislating Immorality: The Homosexual Movement Comes Out of the Closet.* Franklin, TN: Moody Press and Legacy Communications, 1993.
Dean Hamer and Peter Copeland	*The Science of Desire: The Search for the Gay Gene and the Biology of Behavior.* New York: Simon & Schuster, 1994.
Daniel Harris	*The Rise and Fall of Gay Culture.* New York: Hyperion, 1997.
Keith Hartman	*Congregations in Conflict: The Battle over Homosexuality.* New Brunswick, NJ: Rutgers University Press, 1997.
John F. Harvey	*The Truth About Homosexuality: The Cry of the Faithful.* San Francisco: Ignatius Press, 1998.
Didi Herman	*The Antigay Agenda: Orthodox Vision and the Christian Right.* Chicago: University of Chicago Press, 1997.
Ann Heron, ed.	*Two Teenagers in Twenty: Writings by Gay and Lesbian Youth.* Boston: Alyson, 1995.
Mark Hertzog	*The Lavender Vote: Lesbians, Gay Men, and Bisexuals in American Electoral Politics.* New York: New York University Press, 1996.
Richard Isay	*Becoming Gay: The Journey to Self-Acceptance.* New York: Pantheon Press, 1996.
Mark D. Jordan	*The Invention of Sodomy in Christian Theology.* Chicago: University of Chicago Press, 1998.
Martin Kantor	*Homophobia: Description, Development, and Dynamics of Gay Bashing.* Westport, CT: Praeger, 1998.
Morris B. Kaplan	*Sexual Justice: Democratic Citizenship and the Politics of Desire.* New York: Routledge, 1997.
Jonathan Ned Katz	*The Invention of Heterosexuality.* New York: Dutton, 1995.
James E. Kennedy	*About Face: A Gay Officer's Account of How He Stopped Prosecuting Gays in the Army and Started Fighting for Their Rights.* Secaucus, NJ: Birch Lane Press, 1995.
Fritz Klein	*The Bisexual Option.* Binghamton, NY: Haworth Press, 1995.
Jeff Konrad	*You Don't Have to Be Gay.* Hilo, HI: Pacific Publishing House, 1992.
Simon LeVay	*Queer Science: The Use and Abuse of Research into Homosexuality.* Cambridge, MA: MIT Press, 1996.

Simon LeVay and
Elisabeth Nonas

City of Friends: A Portrait of the Gay and Lesbian Community in America. Cambridge, MA: MIT Press, 1995.

Tony Marco

Gay Rights: A Public Health Disaster and Civil Wrong. Fort Lauderdale, FL: Coral Ridge Ministries, 1992.

Adam Mastoon

The Shared Heart: Portraits and Stories Celebrating Lesbian, Gay, and Bisexual Young People. New York: William Morrow, 1997.

Brian McNaught

Gay Issues in the Workplace. New York: St. Martin's Press, 1993.

John J. McNeill

The Church and the Homosexual. Boston: Beacon Press, 1993.

Francis Mark
Mondimore

A Natural History of Homosexuality. Baltimore: Johns Hopkins University Press, 1996.

Timothy F. Murphy

Gay Science: The Ethics of Sexual Orientation Research. New York: Columbia University Press, 1997.

Michael Nava and
Robert Dawidoff

Created Equal: Why Gay Rights Matter to America. New York: St. Martin's Press, 1994.

Joseph Nicolosi

Reparative Therapy of Male Homosexuality. Northvale, NJ: Jason Aronson, 1991.

Saul M. Olyan and
Martha Craven
Nussbaum, eds.

Sexual Orientation and Human Rights in American Religious Discourse. New York: Oxford University Press, 1998.

Deb Price and
Joyce Murdoch

And Say Hi to Joyce: America's First Gay Column Comes Out. New York: Doubleday, 1995.

Gary Remafedi

Death by Denial: Studies of Suicide in Gay and Lesbian Teenagers. Boston: Alyson, 1994.

Gabriel Rotello

Sexual Ecology: AIDS and the Destiny of Gay Men. New York: Penguin, 1998.

Thomas E. Schmidt

Straight and Narrow? Compassion and Clarity in the Homosexuality Debate. Farmington, PA: Plough Books, 1998.

Lois Shawver

And the Flag Was Still There: Straight People, Gay People, and Sexuality in the U.S. Military. Binghamton, NY: Haworth Press, 1995.

Michelangelo Signorile

Queer in America: Sex, the Media, and the Closets of Power. New York: Anchor Books, 1994.

Diane Silver

The New Civil War: The Lesbian and Gay Struggle for Civil Rights. Danbury, CT: Franklin Watts, 1997.

Charles W. Socarides

Homosexuality: A Freedom Too Far. Phoenix: Adam Margrave Books, 1995.

Arlene Stein	*Sex and Sensibility: Stories of a Lesbian Generation.* Berkeley and Los Angeles: University of California Press, 1997.
William Stewart and Emily Hamer, eds.	*Cassell's Queer Companion: A Dictionary of Lesbian and Gay Life and Culture.* New York: Cassell Academic, 1995.
John R.W. Stott	*Same-Sex Partnerships: A Christian Perspective.* Grand Rapids, MI: Fleming H. Revell, 1998.
Mark P. Strasser	*Legally Wed: Same-Sex Marriage and the Constitution.* Ithaca, NY: Cornell University Press, 1997.
Andrew Sullivan	*Virtually Normal: An Argument About Homosexuality.* New York: Knopf, 1995.
Andrew Sullivan, ed.	*Same-Sex Marriage: Pro and Con.* New York: Vintage Books, 1997.
Edward Taussig	*501 Great Things About Being Gay.* Kansas City, MO: Andrews & McMeel, 1998.
Dan Woog	*School's Out: The Impact of Gay and Lesbian Issues on American Schools.* Boston: Alyson, 1995.
Urvashi Vaid	*Virtual Equality: The Mainstreaming of Gay and Lesbian Liberation.* New York: Anchor Books, 1995.
Steven Zeeland	*Sailors and Sexual Identity: Crossing the Line Between "Straight" and "Gay" in the U.S. Navy.* Binghamton, NY: Haworth Press, 1995.

INDEX